MAKE SURE IT'S DEDUCTIBLE

MAKE SURE IT'S DEDUCTIBLE

Little-known tax tips for your small business

EVELYN JACKS

 McGraw-Hill
Ryerson

Toronto Montréal New York Burr Ridge Bangkok Bogotá Caracas
Lisbon London Madrid Mexico City Milan New Delhi Seoul
Singapore Sydney Taipei

McGraw-Hill
Ryerson Limited
*A Subsidiary of The **McGraw·Hill** Companies*

This edition, published in 1999, has been carefully researched and verified for accuracy; however, due to the complexity of the subject matter and the continual changes occurring in the subject matter, neither the author nor the publisher can be held responsible for errors or omissions, or consequences of any actions resulting from information in this book. Examples discussed are intended as general guidelines only, contain fictional names and characters and any resemblance to real persons or events is purely coincidental. The reader is urged to seek the services of a competent and experienced professional should further guidance in income tax preparation be required.

ISBN 0-07-560543-0
1 2 3 4 5 6 7 8 9 0 GTC 8 7 6 5 4 3 2 1 0 9

Canadian Cataloguing in Publication Data

Jacks, Evelyn, 1955-
    Make sure it's deductible: little-known tax tips for your small business

(SOHO solutions for Canadians)
Includes index.
ISBN 0-07-560543-0

1. Small business – Taxation – Law and legislation – Canada – Popular works. 2. Income tax planning – Law and legislation – Canada – Popular works. I. Title. II. Series.

HJ4662.A45J32 1999   343.7105'.268   C99-930390-2

Publisher: **Joan Homewood**
Production Coordinator: **Susanne Penny**
Editor: **Rachel Mansfield**
Electronic Page Composition: **Lynda Powell**
Cover Design: **Sharon Matthews**
Printed and bound in Canada

··

For My Mom

Now, it is time for you.
May happiness and contentment
Fill the rest of your days,
And the warmth of knowing
Your invaluable contribution
To the life, health and happiness
Of those around you,
Will always be appreciated
And never forgotten.

Love,
Ev.

Table of Contents

Introduction

A progressive tax system is one which promotes the ideals of fairness and equity, simplicity and compliance. Unfortunately some of these ideals are at odds with one another, as illustrated below:

- our tax system is based on self-assessment: taxpayers are expected to voluntarily comply with the requirement to file a tax return, correctly assess taxes owing and pay them on time
- taxpayers expect equity: that others in like circumstances pay similar taxation levels
- to be completely fair, however, one must put into place special provisions for special groups of people—the sick and the disabled, the elderly, families, business people and investors
- the fairer the tax system, the more complex it will be
- complexity, often caused by the quest for fairness, can make compliance difficult
- without compliance there is no equity.

You can see what we mean.

As a result, it is not necessarily true that two neighbours, each earning gross revenues of, let's say, $50,000, will pay the same level of tax. In fact, it's not always income level that determines the after-tax result. . . it's income *source* that will have the biggest bearing on your family's welfare over the long run, a fact that few Canadians have considered seriously.

What's more, the type of income earned, when it's earned, and by whom, together with the application of generous rules for the expenses of earning certain income sources, will determine your family's after-tax status.

Take Jean-Paul, for example, a 35-year-old self-employed electrical contractor, who suffered through a devastating divorce over a year ago. You could see the pain on his face as he spoke of missing his eight-year-old son, who moved with his mom to a small town over four hours away. His commitment to the boy was unfaltering. Every weekend he drove the four-hour trek to visit with his son, and then back home again.

"It's worth it to see my boy," Jean-Paul sighed, " but I am exhausted and the travelling is costing me a fortune. Is there any way I could write some of this off?"

At first glance, the answer would be no. Driving to and from the small town to visit one's own child is considered to be a personal expense; not deductible.

But wait. Jean-Paul was self-employed. Did he ever bid on work in the area in which his child lived? No. Could he? Yes. In fact, a new school was expected to be built in the vicinity very soon. Was it too late to bid on the work? No.

Jean-Paul could now legitimately write off the cost of driving to and from the town in which the work would be completed. Trips to place the bid, negotiate with the parties, supervise his work crew, etc., would all qualify for expense deductibility. So would the hotel bills he incurred to perform the work. His travel now had a dual purpose. Deductibility of at least a portion of the trip could be justified to Revenue Canada, as there was a reasonable expectation of profit in the future.

Only a few miles away, driving for visits with his son would be considered a personal expense. But Jean-Paul took this into account when filing his tax return, and accomplished his goals: the majority of his expenses were now tax deductible, leaving more in his pocket to spend on his beloved son. He now makes a point of looking for work in the area over the weekends, so that he can better balance business and personal resources.

Often, taxpayers can increase their tax write-offs, without dramatically changing their lifestyles. It's all in the way you think about the time and money you have. If you can make a business case for the expenditure — even if you have to prorate the cost for a personal component — the after-tax benefits will accumulate in double-digit yields.

That's the purpose behind this little book — to urge you to re-evaluate your existing income sources and annual expenditures. Is there a business purpose to any of them? Could there be? If so, what do you have to do to conform to Revenue Canada's audit requirements to ensure their acceptance? How can you plan to make decisions throughout the year to enhance your lifestyle with increased after-tax dollars. How can you be more astute and vigilant about claiming every tax deduction and credit you are entitled to?

With marginal tax costs in the range of 26% to over 50% of every dollar you earn, it makes absolute "cents" to aggressively pursue your legal rights to arrange your affairs within the framework of Canadian tax law so as to pay the least amount of tax possible. You *can* take control of the taxes you pay! Make the decision today to take a fresh look at your next financial commitment and. . .

. . . *Make Sure It's Deductible*!

CHAPTER 1

Key Reasons Why Canadians Pay Too Much Tax

"The greatest discovery of my generation is that human beings can alter their lives by altering their attitudes of mind."
WILLIAM JAMES

KEY CONCEPTS

- There are 10 key reasons why Canadians overpay their taxes
- One way to reduce taxes and build wealth is to start an unincorporated small business
- Tax-deductible expenditures must first occur to produce taxable income in the future
- Small business owners face an ever-present potential for audit
- Business owners must be prepared to show a reasonable expectation of profit from their commercial activities over a period of time
- A knowledge of tax provisions is key in the decisions a business owner makes throughout the year.

REAL LIFE: David groaned as he completed this year's tax return. He thought he was doing well, supporting his family on his $40,000 of employment income. David scrutinized his simple tax return: one T4 slip and not much else. He had paid over $8,000 in taxes this year, and his take-home pay of about $2,600 a month barely seemed to cover all the expenses of running a household with a stay-at-home mom and two small kids. How could this be? David, a typical Canadian dad, wondered whether he needed a second job, or perhaps, a self-employment opportunity.

THE PROBLEM

Canadians who pay too much tax face the following challenges. They:

- Earn the majority of their income from one source (i.e., employment or pensions)
- Have one person in the family who earns significantly more than the others
- Pay too much to the government through tax withholding or tax instalments
- Look at tax filing on an annual basis only
- Fail to build equity
- Have no saving and/or estate planning goals
- Have trouble keeping records
- Don't know themselves, their investments or their business well enough
- Don't effectively communicate their current and future tax and financial affairs to their professional advisors; fail to ask effective questions about current and future tax-savings planning, and/or fail to demand the answers to help themselves make tax-wise decisions.

THE SOLUTION

Today there are over 3.5 million small businesses in Canada who report over $27 billion in gross income, according to Revenue Canada's most recent taxation statistics. They are small business owners of every type: professionals, commission salespersons, farmers, fishermen, and revenue property owners. They are people who invest their time and money first, to reap the rewards of profit and equity in their enterprises later. In fact, ownership of a small business in Canada today can have both: tax advantages, and the potential to substantially increase the results of their personal time and efforts over the long term. That's because they have numerous opportunities to do the following:

- Diversify their income sources
- Split income with family members, and thereby reduce their overall rate of tax on income
- Increase their working capital by reducing or eliminating the withholding taxes the government takes from gross income sources
- Decrease personal living costs by writing off the business portion of personal expenses
- Average their tax costs over a period of years
- Build equity within the goodwill of their business
- Take pro-active control of their retirement income and their estate.

In order to reap the benefits of these opportunities however, the small business owner must understand the rules of the tax-filing game. That includes an understanding of the relationship the self-employed have with the tax department. These concepts will be discussed throughout this book. But first, some preliminary comments to help you prepare to save tax dollars through your new business venture.

THE PARAMETERS

In order to take advantage of the benefits provided to the self-employed under the law, a new approach must be taken to the tax-filing ritual. Three basic parameters must be observed:

Take a Broader View of Your Tax and Financial Affairs   The small business owner must look not only at his/her own individual return, but to the returns of each family member as an extension of the economic activities produced within the family unit, in the current year and over a period of years.

Guard and Grow Your Source of Income From the Business   To make sure your claims for expenditures made to start and grow your business are deductible, a specific requirement must be met. That is, it's not enough to simply start an economic activity, no matter how simple or small. One must start earning *income* from it, now *or in the future.* That's the key. Those who can show earnings from a new source of income from their commercial activities, legitimize the deductions they are allowed under the Income Tax Act. That revenue source will help to prove that your business has *a reasonable expectation of profit.*

Focus on Reducing Average Annual Tax Costs Over a Period of Time Earning business revenues is a process that evolves over time and takes into account certain risk factors: that income depends on the results achieved at the end of a contract. This is a distinct difference from the earning of employment income, which occurs regularly, and generally without risk. In fact, the employee need not worry about the risk that revenues might not be collected due to uncontrollable factors like bad debts, damage to equipment or the misfortunes of those with whom you have made a contract for income. Therefore, the tax-filing profile of the self-employed requires an assessment of profitability over time. The story of the *evolution of the business* is paramount in assessing tax costs. The Income Tax Act recognizes this evolutionary income-producing process by providing flexibility in claiming the deductions for expenditures of the business. These rules will be discussed in detail in subsequent chapters. You should know now, though, that this very flexibility provides a risk factor to the taxpayer: business losses can be disallowed retroactively — despite the fact that claims are fully supported by documentation — based on a subjective analysis: whether a reasonable expectation of profit exists.

Because the self-employed are subject to a greater risk of scrutiny by tax auditors, it is important to understand basic tax-filing parameters before embarking on a new small business organization. A brief summary follows:

Who Files a Return?

Canadian residents must report their taxable income to the government annually. Your obligation to file a Canadian tax return usually ends when you leave the country permanently, unless you continue to earn certain Canadian-source income after you leave, including Canadian Business Income.

What's Taxable Income?

For Canadian residents, that's world-wide income, in Canadian funds, after allowable deductions. You should also know that income sources are classified and subject to varying tax treatment. In other words, not all income is taxed in the same manner, and that can have advantages for the taxpayer who diversifies income sources.

How is Employment Income Taxed?

Income and deductions from employment, including salary, wages, gratuities, bonuses and vacation pay, are specifically defined and outlined in the Income Tax Act, leaving little room for flexibility or interpretation. Income must be reported on the return in the year received, and includes non-cash benefits and employee stock options.

Can Employees Claim Tax Deductions?

Sometimes, yes. Employees, however, may not take tax deductions for any expenditures except those listed by the Act; even if the taxpayer legitimately makes the expenditure in pursuit of his/her duties from an office or employment. A good example of these restrictions concerns the acquisition of tools or equipment, computers or cell phones. An employee may not claim a deduction for Capital Cost Allowance or leasing costs on any assets except motor vehicles, aircraft or musical instruments.

Another example concerns the deductibility of meals consumed by the employee while away on company business: that employee must be absent from the employer's place of business for a period of not less than 12 hours in order to claim his/her meal expenses. Further, to claim any deductible expenses, a certificate signed by the employer (Form T2200, *Declaration of Employment Conditions*) must be available for Revenue Canada to verify that the employee was required, under the employment contract, to pay the tax-deductible expenses being claimed, and was not reimbursed for the costs.

How is the Income of the Self-Employed Taxed?

The Income Tax Act states that a taxpayer's income for the year from a business or property is the taxpayer's "profit." This word is not specifically defined in the Act, but does infer that the activity conducted has a business purpose. It encompasses the concept that those expenditures that cause the taxpayer's gross income to be reduced to the taxable net income are legitimate, provided that they have an income-earning purpose and are not personal in nature. Professionals will look to Generally Accepted Accounting Principles (GAAP) as defined in the Canadian Institute of Chartered Accountants' *CICA Handbook*, in computing profits.

However, sometimes the Act itself sets out exceptions to those rules. For example, the deduction for meals and entertainment expenses is usually limited to 50% of their cost. Most importantly, the income or loss a taxpayer reports on the tax return can be challenged by Revenue Canada if there is no "reasonable expectation of profit" over time from the business venture. This is a "grey area" of interpretation that has led to hundreds of challenges in the courts (for a discussion, see Chapter 11). It is particularly problematic because the creation of a source of income generally results from the pursuit of profit. Despite this, the onus is always on the self-employed taxpayer to show that a legitimate source of taxable income exists from the activities of the business, either now or in the future, in order to ensure the deductibility of the costs of pursuing that income.

It is also important to understand that the Income Tax Act separates the sources of income from a business — which is actively pursued — from sources of income from "property," which occurs with only a passive effort by the taxpayer. Income from property generally includes dividends, employee profit-sharing plans, retirement compensation arrangements, income from royalties, interest from investment contracts, income from annuities, recaptured depreciation on equipment dispositions, capital gains, and shareholder benefits.

What Deductions Can Be Claimed by the Self-Employed?

Here is the general rule for claiming deductions of a small business: if you can show that your expenditures were made or incurred to produce income, now or in the foreseeable future, and the amount of the expenditure was reasonable, Revenue Canada must allow the claim. However, this is also where the concept of "onus of proof" arises: it is your responsibility to show both potential for profit now or in the future and reasonableness in all documentation.

This includes the deduction for interest expenses. In the case of those who borrow funds to invest in their enterprises or property, it is important to note that there must be potential for income from the property — profits, rents, dividends or interest — for the interest amounts to be deductible at all.

You should also know that "capital appreciation" is not considered to be business income. That's important.

How Is Capital Appreciation Taxed?

The Income Tax Act states that only $3/4$ of capital gains received in the year must be included as income, and that these gains can be offset by $3/4$ of capital losses of the current year, or any prior year since 1972.

There are certain tax-free exceptions to this rule, which include gains on the sale of the principal residence, the reporting of gains when replacement properties are acquired, and tax-free rollovers to children and/or spouses in certain cases.

Striving to earn income from the disposition of capital assets is wise. The reason? Asset appreciation is never taxed until disposition, which can include sale, gift, conversion to personal use, or disposition by way of emigration or death. Then, gains usually qualify for a tax exemption of 25%. Also, except in the case of death, you do have some control over when you sell or otherwise dispose of an asset. For example, you could reduce your tax burden by disposing of the asset over two tax years (half in December, half in January) or by offsetting capital gains in the year with capital losses, and so on.

TAX ADVISOR

Before any taxpayer begins a new small business, it is important to go through an assessment procedure. Start this procedure as follows:

Complete a Current Year Tax Review

Prepare a Tax Summary to confirm how current income sources are earned and taxed. A sample plan, prepared on the CANTAX tax preparation software, is on page 8, for Linda Baker, who started a small business on the side last year. Due to her operating loss, she has a tax refund, and note that she has some real potential tax savings in her future with her unused RRSP contribution room of $3,722.

Analyze Current RRSP Contribution Room

The RRSP will become an anchor for tax deferral and retirement savings for you. The example on page 9 shows Linda Baker's RRSP Planner. You can see that it will save her about $913 in taxes or 25% for each dollar invested this year.

Know Your Current Average And Marginal Tax Rates on Each Income Type

In Linda's case, her employment income, as well as her net business income will be taxed at a rate of about 24%; while dividends earned will attract just over 6% in taxes, and capital gains, about 18% (see page 10).

Prepare a Tax Review for Each Family Member

One of the objectives you should have whenever you file a tax return is to attempt to reduce taxes not just for each individual, but for the family unit as a whole. You should look into the legitimate ways to split income with family members, take advantage of transferable deductions and credits, and tax deferral opportunities.

Assess Previous Errors and Omissions

Because a small business owner is subject to greater scrutiny by tax auditors, it is important for you to clean up any past filing problems with Revenue Canada before you start your business. For example, if you have failed to file tax returns in the past, you may wish to consider filing them now. Revenue Canada may owe you money with regard to overpaid taxes at source, or refundable tax credits you may be eligible for. If you had eligible earned income in those years, you will also create increased RRSP contribution room, which Revenue Canada will not yet have calculated.

Remember, if you voluntarily comply with the law, you will avoid gross negligence and tax evasion penalties. It is always important to clear up your tax-filing status, and it could pay off for you in the future.

Sample 1.1 Tax Summary

Name of taxpayer	Social Insurance Number	
LINDA BAKER	123-123-123	**DRAFT**

1998 Tax Return Summary

Identification

Paper filed

C/O:		Marital status:	Married
Street:	23 PLEASANT VALLEY DRIVE	Spouse:	JOHN
City:	BURLINGHAM	Spouse's SIN:	667-554-889
Prov:	ON	Spouse's net income:	55,000.00
Code:	M5T 0V6	CTB credit:	
Phone:	905-430-5788	Apply for GSTC?	No
Birthdate:	02/02/1955	GST credit:	

Total income

Employment income				101	25,000	00
Business income	Gross	162	10,000 00	Net 135	-4,320	60
			Total income	150	20,679	40

Net income

	Net Income	236	20,679	40

Taxable income

	Taxable Income	260	20,679	40

Non-refundable tax credits

Basic personal amount	300	6,456	00
Canada or Quebec Pension Plan contributions through employment	308	688	00
Employment Insurance premiums from box 18 on all T4 slips	312	675	00
Total non-refundable credits 335		7,819	00
Multiply the amount on line 335 by 17% = 338		1,329	23
Total non-refundable tax credits 350		1,329	23

Refund or Balance owing

Federal Tax	406	2,186	27
Federal individual surtax	419		32 79
Net federal tax 420		2,219	07
tax	428	934	63
Total payable 435		(3,153 70)

15% of Taxable Income

Total income tax deducted	437	4,500	00
Total credits.	482	4,500	00	4,500	00
Line 435 minus line 482			-1,346	30
Refund	484		1,346	30

1999 RRSP Contribution Limit	(3,722 29)

Courtesy of CANTAX Tax Preparation Software.

Sample 1.2	Current RRSP Contribution Room

Name of taxpayer	Social Insurance Number	
LINDA BAKER	123-123-123	**DRAFT**

Family RRSP/RRIF Investment Planner - Page 1

1999 RRSP Contribution Planner

RRSP room (maximum deduction) for 1999	3,722 29
Over-contribution limit	2,000 00
Maximum RRSP contribution for 1999	5,722 29
Unclaimed contributions from prior years	0 00
Maximum amount to be contributed for 1999	5,722 29

Projected contributions:

to December 31, 1999	0 00
to March 1, 2000	0 00
Monthly: 477 00 X 12 months	5,724 00
Total projected contributions	5,724 00

Clawback Reductions

Income Type	Projected Clawback	Projected RRSP Contribution	Clawback After RRSP	Amount Saved
OAS	0 00	5,724 00	0 00	0 00
EI	0 00	5,724 00	0 00	0 00

Total Tax Savings (including decrease in claw-back)

If you were to contribute	3,722 29	or more to your RRSP in 1999 your savings will be	912 94	**25%**
If you were to contribute	5,724 00	to your RRSP in 1999 your savings will be	912 94	

Additional Savings Through Increase in Family Benefits and Refundable Tax Credits

Income Type	Projected Credit	Projected RRSP Contribution	Credit After RRSP	Amount Saved
Child Tax Benefit	0 00	5,724 00	0 00	0 00
GST Credit	0 00	5,724 00	0 00	0 00
Refundable Med. Sup	0 00	5,724 00	0 00	0 00
Prov. Tax Credits	0 00	5,724 00	0 00	0 00
Total	0 00		0 00	0 00

Growth potential - the power of compounding

The sooner you start the better!
Compare the RRSP balance at retirement if you start saving now or wait for 10 years:

Starting age	43	53
Yearly contribution	1,000 00	1,000 00
Rate of return.	0.00 %	0.00 %
Balance at age 65	22,000 00	12,000 00

Courtesy of CANTAX Tax Preparation Software.

Sample 1.3 — Average and Marginal Tax Rates

Name of taxpayer	Social Insurance Number	
LINDA BAKER	123-123-123	DRAFT

Investment Tax Planner

Marginal tax rate planner

Current income sources	Amount	Average Tax Rate	Marginal Tax Rate
Employment Income	25,000 00	14.85	23.88
Interest income	0 00	14.85	23.88
Canadian dividends (actual)	0 00	14.85	6.43
Capital gains (actual)	0 00	14.85	17.91
Rental income	0 00	14.85	23.88
Business income	-4,320 60	14.85	23.88
Other income	0 00	14.85	23.88

Non-registered Investment rate of return planner

Desired rate of return on non-registered investment portfolio	10.00
Required pre-tax earnings at your current income level:	
on interest income	13.14
on Canadian dividend income	10.69
on capital gains	12.18
on other type of income	13.14

Pre-tax income diversification planner

Future income sources	Amount	Average Tax Rate	Marginal Tax Rate
Employment income	30,000 00	20.42	36.53
Interest income	450 00	20.42	36.53
Canadian dividends (actual)	500 00	20.42	22.24
Capital gains (actual)	500 00	20.42	27.40
Rental income	0 00	20.42	36.53
Business income	5,000 00	20.42	36.53
Other income	0 00	20.42	36.53
Total Income:	36,450 00	**Total Taxes:**	7,441.99

Action Plan

1.
2.
3.
4.
5.

Courtesy of CANTAX Tax Preparation Software.

For example, you may have to rely on Revenue Canada's Fairness Committee to grant you a waiver of interest and penalties should a severe hardship occur in your circumstances in the future. More on that later.

And, if you find you have missed an important provision in your prior filed returns — like medical expenses, charitable donations, disability tax credits, safety deposit box charges, or moving expenses — file Form T1 ADJ to request an adjustment. You can do so all the way back to 1985 for most federal provisions.

Plan to Tax Cost Average

Once you have all the steps above in place, you can integrate tax efficiency into your normal business planning activities. In fact, you can plan to average your tax costs for the current year, the prior years, and future years, by applying the provisions available to you within the Income Tax Act. We'll show you how in Chapter 2, How to Tax Cost Average.

RECAP: How To Get Ready To Save Money On Your Taxes

1. **Prepare a current tax profile assessment:** Ask your tax advisor to assess your current tax-filing profile. What you want to know is how your current income sources are being taxed. Make sure you know what your marginal tax rates are on all new dollars earned in the future.

2. **Find new money:** Many people overpay their taxes every year, and then fail to go back and ask for a refund due to errors and omissions on their returns. This is possible by requesting a formal adjustment to prior-filed returns — all the way back to 1985! Ask your tax advisor to do a thorough prior-filing review for each family member. This is particularly important if you have been changing advisors from year to year, or have missed filing tax returns in any prior years. Make sure you ask for your overpaid dollars back, if applicable.

3. **Launch future RRSP tax savings:** Make sure you isolate the ways to reduce future taxes now. One way to do this is to have your tax advisor prepare an RRSP contribution room analysis for each family member. You'll want to carry forward undeducted contributions in cases where income is too low to derive a benefit from the RRSP contribution. Where income levels are high, make sure RRSP deductions are taken. You'll want to receive a tax refund for every dollar contributed, as this new money can be used to finance your business or personal expenses.

4. **Prepare to tax cost average:** Small business owners have the opportunity to average their tax costs over time with specific carry-over provisions. Some carry-over provisions are available to taxpayers in general. Those are the ones to isolate and record now. Examples are prior capital and non-capital loss balances, unclaimed moving expenses or unused medical expenses and charitable donations.

5. **Do some tax planning R & D:** Self-employment is perhaps the ultimate opportunity for income diversification; first from the operations of the enterprise; second, by building a potentially saleable concern. Talk to your tax advisor about your proposed business plans, your business structure and receive information about obligations to Revenue Canada, for income taxes, source deductions and GST/HST remittances, as well as business name licensing, trademark applications and the like.

6. **Plan to split business income with family members:** By starting a home-based business, you have the potential to reap double-digit returns in tax savings, simply by giving family members an opportunity to work for you. Try not to earn all the profits yourself. Find tasks within your business that can be delegated to others; then consider employing family members who are willing to take on the job a stranger would normally be hired for, and pay them at fair market value.

7. **Be vigilant about keeping track of all expenditures:** Small business owners can reap double-digit tax savings on each dollar they spend in their small business ventures, depending on their province of residence and income levels. Keep track of all money spent in the establishment of your business enterprise, even if you are not yet operating. Some of these start-up costs may be tax deductible.

8. **Get ready to give birth to your business.** Remember that a small business must be born and then nurtured to grow into a profitable entity. Both money and time must be expended in advance for revenues to begin to flow. This involves the injection of capital and the formalization of the financial path your business will take to its maturity. Revenue Canada will want to know the details of birth and growth when assessing your claims. Keep track of all initiatives that precede the revenue flow in your business.

....

CHAPTER 2

How to Tax Cost Average

"We make our habits, and then our habits make us."
JOHN DYDEN

KEY CONCEPTS

- By looking at your tax-filing profile over a 10-year period, you can average your tax costs
- Reduce the taxes you pay by diversifying income sources and claiming every tax deduction you're entitled to
- You can save certain permissive deductions for use in future years when income is higher
- Income splitting with family members can help reduce the overall taxes you pay on net business revenues
- You can control the taxes you pay with a detailed tax and business plan.

REAL LIFE: How would you like to save tens of thousands of dollars in taxes over the next several years? What would you do with the extra money? How would it change your life? The good news is that it's possible, you can do it and it's easy. In fact, this recently happened to Mary, a single entrepreneur living in Ontario.

Unable to afford their dream camping trip to beautiful BC, prompted by her boyfriend, Mary decided to have her tax advisor prepare a current year tax review. Perhaps there was something she was missing out on by filing her own return. Mary makes $40,000 a year from her efforts as a manufacturers agent, which is shown on the T4A slip sent to her at the end of the year. She reports the amounts as self-employment income on her tax return, and that's it, she's done. "A simple return," she'll say every year; "no hassles."

Turns out, Mary's erroneous self-assessment has extracted a costly fee. She is dramatically overpaying her taxes. In preparing her return as she described it — which is perfectly legal and correct, by the way — she owes over $11,000 at year end. Let's project that liability forward for a moment. Should her income stay constant over the next ten years, she'll have paid about $111,000 in taxes — more than what's left to pay on her home mortgage.

In addition, because the annual amount she owes the government at year end is over $2,000, she is required to make quarterly tax instalment payments throughout the year. This will take approximately $2,800 out of her pocket *every calendar quarter*. What does this mean to Mary's lifestyle? No holidays this summer. . .fall, winter, or spring.

THE PROBLEM

Most people overpay their taxes year in and year out because they think about their tax liabilities only once a year. . .at tax-filing time. Unfortunately, at this point you are usually only reconciling history. Aside from maximizing every tax deduction and credit you and your family are entitled to, there are few proactive measures available to reduce the tax burden of the tax year in question.

In fact, the difference between a "taxpayer" and a "tax saver" lies in the desire to gain control of his/her future tax bill. A Tax Saver takes on the task of controlling the amount of taxes being paid to the government over a period of years — looking back and forward — to get a new result: a tax cost that on average is significantly lower than the current liability.

It is the self-employed who are in the best position to minimize tax in this way, largely through the creation of a variety of income sources and offsetting deductions. As discussed in Chapter 1, business income, which is generally taxed within the calendar year, can be reduced by all reasonable expenses incurred to earn income from a venture that has a reasonable expectation of profit. Employees, on the other hand, are limited to writing off only a very specific group of expenses, and then only with the certification of their employers.

So the Tax Saver's goal is to reduce the taxes paid now and over the long term, to avoid one of the taxpayer's greatest risks: the real dollar cost of under-utilizing available and legitimate tax provisions.

THE SOLUTION

The key to reducing the taxes you pay is to put yourself and your family in the position of controlling income type, when it's earned, who reports it and how much of it is subject to tax. Your goal is to create an effective plan to increase after-tax wealth, implemented over a period of years, within the framework of the law. One way to do this is to *tax cost average*.

Your *tax cost* is the real dollars you send to Revenue Canada every year. If you net $40,000 a year from your small business, for example, your tax cost for the year will be just over $11,000, (the exact amount depends on your province of residence).

Tax cost averaging is the calculated use of existing tax provisions to reduce the taxes you pay *over a period of years*. This involves the diversification of income sources, the application of all existing tax provisions to reduce your current tax bill, and the maximization of carry-over provisions to average out the good years and the bad.

Tax cost averaging begins with a *Tax Savings Blueprint*. The Tax Saver starts on the road to after-tax profits by understanding how various income sources are earned and taxed. This can best be illustrated with the preparation of a multi-year overview; one that anticipates income amounts and sources, deductions and taxation rates over a period of time, preferably a 10-year period. This can be a tricky, but worthwhile endeavour.

The Tax Savings Blueprint is like a business plan. . .it defines and structures your after-tax results and how you are going to achieve them in advance. Anticipating change within your tax-filing portfolio over a ten-year period can help you maximize all available tax provisions that apply to your changing personal situation, which in turn can pay handsome returns — five and six figures for some — over your productive lifetime.

You see, the opportunity for tax savings arises out of change. Yes, it's true; tax law does change at least once (but usually several times) throughout the tax year. This is why taxpayers often lose their sense of control over their affairs. . .who has the time to study all the draft legislation anyway? Your tax professionals do, and you should consult them for a regular update.

But it's the change within your personal affairs that matters the most. You are the one in control of those changes, and you can play out your tax-filing strategies accordingly.

In short, it is knowing the law, and then applying it properly to your current personal and financial affairs over a period of years that will bring results in the form of significant tax savings.

THE TAX ADVISOR

Mary was delighted to find out about the tax cost averaging process when she visited her tax advisor. He showed her how to reclaim some control over her tax costs. She hadn't known, for example, about the allowable claims for:

- automobile expenses
- workplace in the home expenses
- operating expenses, like promotions and travelling expenses
- RRSP deductions, to maximize her RRSP room.

He then illustrated the financial results available to a better-informed tax filer. A quick look over her loosely kept books and records revealed the following:

- auto expenses are $2,500 after taking personal driving into account
- home office expenses are $1,200: after personal-use allocation
- other operating expenses $3,500
- Mary has made an effort to contribute $2,000 to her RRSP, yet undeducted, and has RRSP contribution room of $19,500.

The result of including these legitimate claims in her tax-filing profile? A tax bill that's almost $3,000 lower in just one tax year. Over ten years, that amounts to over $30,000! What a way for Mary to produce new capital, without working any harder.

But there's more good news. Now that Mary has produced new money with proper application of the tax provisions that have been waiting for her, we find she's just struck the tip of the tax savings iceberg. For example:

- Mary's quarterly tax instalment payments have been reduced to just over $2,000, a saving of $800 a quarter. Mary can now afford at least one holiday this year.
- She surprises herself with her next decision. She will forego the camping trip to BC this year (much to her boyfriend's chagrin) and instead invest her tax savings in an RRSP, given her plentiful RRSP Room. She finds that by investing the tax savings of $3,000, she'll reap a tax refund that's over $1,000 more next year. . .a perfect way to start saving for a downpayment on the new car she's wanted for years. Besides, that acquisition will give her further tax write-offs against her business income.
- Now, here's another thought. If she takes her RRSP investment and flips it into a Labour Sponsored Venture Capital Fund, she'll get a federal/provincial tax credit of 30%. That's close to yet another $1,000. Now Mary has over $2,000 of new money. . .simply by making some tax-wise decisions. This is fun!
- . . .but wait, maybe she should invest in that new printer for her computer before year end. Her capital cost allowance deduction would then help finance the costs of her office supplies. . .

Get the picture? By using actual business expenses and available RRSP contributions to reduce taxable income, Mary *reduces her average tax cost by over $30,000 in ten years. If she adds the benefits of the Labour Sponsored fund, and the reinvestment of her tax savings in another RRSP, her average tax cost is reduced by over $50,000 over 10 years.*

It is important to see the big picture when it comes to your potential tax savings. Five-figure tax savings returns over a ten-year period are possible for some, and can translate into numerous new investments both inside and outside registered accounts, to send the taxpayer along the road to maximum wealth creation.

THE TAX PARAMETERS

If we've whet your appetite for tax savings, please take a moment now to learn more about the tax theory surrounding the *Tax Cost Averaging* process. Following are a series of parameters to help you understand the benefits of tax cost averaging.

Diversify the Types of Income You Earn Today and in the Future

Here's a quick look at different results brought about by making the decision to earn a variety of different income types. First you should know your approximate federal and provincial tax rates on taxable income. (Ask your tax professional to prepare an exact computation for you, or use your favourite tax software program to do so):

Figure 2.1	Average Personal Tax Rates	
Taxable Income	**Federal Tax Rate**	**Average Federal/Prov. Rate***
Over Basic Personal Amount and Supplement, up to $29,590	17%	26%
$29,591 to $59,180	26%	42%
Over $59,180	29%	50% +

As you can see, those with income levels over $60,000 generally pay the highest marginal tax rates on taxable income levels. . .however, these results will differ from province to province, and with different income types, and the variety of family tax deductions and credits that may apply in each individual case.

What we see in the chart on page 18 is the tax results obtained by a single taxpayer living in Ontario with income at the $40,000 mark; no tax credits other than the Basic Personal Amount and CPP/EI premiums. The example also assumes 100% of the income is earned from the source named. You might be surprised at the completely different tax results obtained from earning the same income but through different sources.

It is interesting to see that income from dividends earned produce the most advantageous tax result at this income level; due to the effects of the dividend tax credit. This credit offsets the gross-up of dividends required under the personal tax system.

* As at time of writing.

Figure 2.2	Approximate Taxes Payable on $40,000 Income				
Income Source	Description	Taxes Payable*	% of $40,000 Earned	Cost of Next $100 Like Income	Marginal Tax Rate
Employment $40,000	Maximum Source Deductions for CPP/EI are made	$ 8,800	22%	$37	37%
Business Inc. $60,000	Net Income of $40,000	$11,100	28%	$36	36%
Taxable Dividends	$40,000 actual dividends grossed up to $50,000	$ 3,600	9%	$22	22%
Capital Gains	3/4 of $40,000 or $30,000	$ 5,700	14%	$28	28%

* 1999 figures, rounded.

Capital gains on the disposition of assets produce the *next* most advantageous tax result. This is because of the 25% tax exemption on the gain itself. In addition, and just as important, you'll never be taxed on your appreciating value until disposition of the asset. That allows you the bonus of accumulating value on a tax-sheltered basis. Finally, should you sell the shares of a qualifying small business corporation or farm property, you could, in fact, qualify for the $500,000 Capital Gains Exemption. . .and a largely tax free capital gain. More on this later.

Watch the CPP "Tax"

The chart shows us that earning $40,000 of net business income costs you the most in real dollars. Why is this? The reason is not so clear: the numbers quoted include the cost of contributing to the Canada Pension Plan, which the unincorporated small business owner must finance entirely. . .a total of $2,373 in 1999. Therefore, tax planning takes on a new dimension for small business owners in the new millennium: every dollar that you can split with family members, or reduce with tax deductions, will reap both tax savings and CPP savings in and around the $37,000 net income level. (On income over this amount, you will have already reached the maximum contribution level, so you won't have to contribute additional premiums.)

The "employer's portion" of the CPP premium the unincorporated small business owner ends up paying for him/herself can usually be written off as a tax deduction for other employees, which reduces net income of the business. However, in the case of a proprietor who is required to contribute for him/herself, only a non-refundable tax credit for the premiums is allowed. This limits the tax benefits for the premium to approximately 26% of the payment; and is not of benefit to you at all if you are *not taxable* in the current year. In fact, in that case, you will want to adjust other areas of your return (perhaps carry forward some of your RRSP contributions, charitable donations and/or medical expenses, for example), to preserve as many tax benefits for the future as possible.

There is yet another way to look at the best use of your RRSP contributions, for those who are taxable on their net business income. For example, we know that CPP rates will be rising now until the year 2003, when they reach a level of 9.9% for combined employer/employee contributions. For the self-employed proprietor, this rate will be applied to the net profits of the business enterprise. But there is a way to reduce this burden; that is, to take a close look at the capital cost allowance claims for business assets.

CCA is taken at the taxpayer's option, and is used to reduce the net income, upon which CPP premiums are based. Given the CPP rate hikes in the future, you may wish to elect to save your CCA deductions, to reduce net business income later as CPP rates rise. Then, to reduce this year's tax liability, you'll want to maximize the use of RRSP contributions, medical expenses, charitable donations and so on. What this illustrates is two different applications of the same tax provisions, for taxpayers with different income scenarios.

Maximize Opportunities to Build Tax-Exempt Income

Many people don't realize that there are certain income sources that, are in fact, completely exempt from tax. They include the following:

- Certain stock option benefits (employees will want to negotiate for these)
- Child Tax Credits, or prepayments, or supplements, and the Child Tax Benefit
- Gifts or inheritances (gifts from employers are generally taxable if over $100)
- Goods and Services Tax payments or prepayments (teenagers should be reminded to file a return for the year they reached age 19 in order to claim this credit for themselves)
- Income received as a personal injury award (income earned as a result of subsequent investment of such sums received by children under age 21 also will not be taxable)
- Life insurance policy proceeds on death of the insured
- Profit from the sale of a person's principal residence.

Taxpayers should strive to arrange their affairs to receive these types of income sources in the future.

Split Income With Family Members

The following chart assumes the taxpayer has an unincorporated small business in the province of Ontario that grosses $125,000 and nets $75,000 after operating expenses. The illustration shows the enormous tax benefits of income splitting. In the first instance, the entire profits are earned by one spouse, while the other spouse has no income. In the second, one spouse is hired to work in the business full time. Salary paid out to that spouse is $37,500.

In the third instance, the profit is really split three ways, as an 18-year-old child of the couple works full-time and draws a salary of $25,000; the spouse works part-time drawing $25,000, and the business owner reports resulting net profits.

As you can see, the family tax liability is almost cut in half with the income-splitting opportunities.

Figure 2.3	The Tax Effect of Income Splitting						
Scenario	Gross Profit	Net Profit	Tax Paid by Owner	Tax Paid by Spouse	Tax Paid by Child	Family Tax Liability	Tax Savings
1	$125,000	$75,000	$24,750	n/a	n/a	$24,750	
2	$125,000	$35,000*	$ 9,200	$7,900	n/a	$17,100	$ 7,650 or **31%**
3	$125,000	$21,700*	$ 4,600	$4,100	$4,100	$12,800	$11,950 or **48%**

* Takes into account the CPP/EI employer's expense, rounded figures for 1999.

Defer Taxation of Income Into the Future

There are several ways to accomplish this:

- Assess which of your potential transactions are taxed on a cash basis and which are taxed on an accrual basis. Capital transactions, for example, are taxed on the cash basis; in the year the transaction actually occurs. Business transactions are generally subject to accrual accounting rules, which require reporting of income as it is earned, rather than when it is received; and expenses when they are incurred, rather than when they are actually paid.
- Time dispositions of assets advantageously, given the cash reporting rules. For example, you might choose to sell your revenue properties strategically if you expect a large taxable gain: one-half in the current

year; one-half in the new year. The same logic could be applied to any capital or depreciable asset.

- In the case of depreciable assets, upon which you expect to pay tax on recapture of previously taken deductions, try to push the disposition into the next taxation year, if the transaction will be happening late in the year, and the buyer is willing to wait.
- When signing contracts for new work in your business, determine whether those contracts should be dated in the new fiscal year, particularly if work on the project will not begin until then.
- Buy mutual funds in the new year, to push any potential distributions into the next taxation year.

Strive to Earn Profits and Build Equity in Making Spending Decisions

Most business owners are so concerned about surviving the day-to-day challenges of making enough money to cover all expenses, that they often forget about the possible rewards, down the road, for the hours of unpaid labour they invest in their businesses in the start-up years. That is, if they build an entity someone else wants to buy in the future, they'll earn a capital gain that could be tax-free in some cases. Below is a true-to-life example.

REAL LIFE: Maggie, a 40-year-old mother, started a cleaning business last year. She started cleaning one house every Friday. After a while her integrity, work ethic and reputation became well known, and within six months Maggie and her staff of three others were cleaning two houses a day, six days a week. After the first year, Maggie was grossing $60,000 a year and taking on even more staff to increase her revenues. Half way through the second year, Maggie was offered $80,000 by a franchise company for her list of clients. She decided to sell her business. Not a bad return for a 24-month effort.

Had Maggie been operating a proprietorship,* she would have reported a gain on goodwill. This would be calculated as $3/4$ of $79,999, as her goodwill would have been considered to be $1.00 when she opened her business. Maggie would add $59,999.25 to her income and pay tax on this amount.

Had this business been incorporated, Maggie would have qualified for the $500,000 Capital Gains Exemption and her gain on the sale of her shares would have been tax-free (note, as some provinces have a net income tax, a slight liability would be calculated there).

* Note: If Maggie had a qualified farm property, the gain may qualify for a Capital Gains Deduction. See Chapter 10.

This scenario begs the question: when should I incorporate? The factors to consider include the following:

- The importance of limited liability to the business owner
- The importance of income diversification: employment income, dividends from after-tax profits, bonuses paid out of the corporation
- Whether there are current year losses. Losses held in a proprietorship offset all other income in the year, the prior three years and for seven years in the future
- The likelihood for a sale of the business .

These issues should be discussed at least annually with your tax advisor. Also see Chapter 10.

Leverage the Cost of Time and Money With Documentation

In our example above, taxpayer Maggie did an excellent job of leveraging time and opportunity for growth. After her own time was filled in, she hired one employee after another, and increasingly spent her time combing the neighbourhood for new houses to clean. The expenses of earning her profits — salaries, car expenses, cleaning supplies, bookkeeping costs and so on — were all tax deductible from her gross earnings. However, proper documentation must be available.

Maggie, who professes no skills for keeping track of receipts or numbers did a wise thing. . .she hired a bookkeeper to do all of that for her. Now she need not fear a tax audit, as her expenses are both legitimate and Maggie can meet the Onus of Proof.

Make Sure You Maximize All Your Eligible Deductions and Credits

The best way to Tax Cost Average is to keep on top of all the most recent tax changes, announced with every federal and provincial budget. As you learn more about our tax system, always go back and review prior-filed returns for any potential errors or omissions. More specifics can be found in Chapters 3 and 4.

Understand the Benefits of Retroactive Tax Adjustments

Revenue Canada may allow an adjustment for some of the unclaimed operating expenses of prior years, but special rules may apply. For example the Capital Cost Allowance deduction will not be allowed, if the adjustment request comes more than 90 days after receiving a Notice of Assessment or Reassessment. However, taxpayers will be able to preserve the claiming of the capital cost allowance deduction for next year in those cases. Home office and operating expenses will likely be allowed, if receipts are provided. If the taxpayer is not claiming a loss, and/or shows that the majority of the income of the year is from the business, the question of "reasonable expectation of profit " will not be an issue. Otherwise, there is always the potential for a more thorough audit, if Revenue Canada suspects abuse. Therefore adjustment requests should never be made carelessly.

Always Have an Up-to-date Record of All Carry-Over Provisions

Business owners and investors do themselves particular harm by not keeping track of all carry-back and carry-forward provisions available over their tax-filing lifetime. Here are some common examples:

- undeducted moving expenses
- undeducted home office expenses
- RRSP carry-forward room or undeducted contributions and undeducted past-service contributions to RPPs
- Capital Gains Deduction availability
- Undepreciated Capital Cost balances
- prior-years' capital and non-capital losses
- undeducted medical expenses
- undeducted charitable donations
- Minimum Tax carry-overs.

TAX ADVISOR

To average out the money you will turn over to Revenue Canada, over the long term, you'll need to be aware of the tax-planning choices available in the past, today, and as time goes by, in the future. It is therefore important to have a good working relationship with a tax professional who clearly understands those tax parameters and how they affect your current and future financial planning goals. Look for a team of professional advisors: accountants, lawyers, financial planner, bankers, life insurance advisors who will inform you of all your options.

Communication with your professionals begins with you, though. Be sure to provide the background information your advisors need to make the best recommendations for you. Here's a way you can facilitate the process:

Chart your tax cost over a ten-year period, using historical data, current year data and projections for the future. At the end of this process, you should receive the following:

- estimated tax calculations for the entire period, using current tax law, and/or known proposals for change
- an analysis of the marginal tax rates paid in the period under the current scenario
- a plan to average-out income, apply deductions and credits, as well as carry-backs and carry-forwards, so as to pay the least amount of tax, at the lowest average rate possible in the period.

RECAP: 10 Action Steps to Ace Tax Cost Averaging

1. **Diversify the types of income you earn** today and in the future, and when you realize it for tax purposes. In this way you can average the taxes charged on your overall income portfolio.

2. **Minimize the CPP Tax.** Take special note of the increasing Canada Pension Plan premium obligations over the next several years and plan your business deductions and income-splitting affairs with this liability in mind.

3. **Build tax-exempt income sources.** Maximize opportunities to receive tax-exempt income now, in the future, and within your estate. This includes investments in tax-exempt principal residences and life insurance policies.

4. **Split income with family members** under all provisions available under the law.

5. **Defer taxation of income** into the future with registered pension and/or education plans and by checking out tax-efficient investment strategies using capital asset acquisitions.

6. **Strive to both earn profits and build equity** in all future business planning decisions.

7. **Leverage the cost of time and money with proper documentation.** . . make sure you miss no tax deductions due to poor bookkeeping skills.

8. **Understand how to make on-going retroactive tax adjustments** and then use them whenever the opportunity arises to reduce previously paid taxes, or to bring forward provisions that will reduce future tax liabilities.

9. **Have an up-to-date record of all carry-over provisions** available for reference at all times, and make sure that if you change accountants the new professional knows about these too.

10. **Make sure your tax-planning activities include a 10-year viewpoint** to fully maximize your tax cost averaging process.

CHAPTER 3

How to Start a Tax-Efficient Small Business

"Ultimately we know deeply that the other side of every fear is a freedom."
MARILYN FERGUSON

KEY CONCEPTS

- A business includes an undertaking of any kind that is not a hobby or for personal enjoyment
- Formalize the business plan, budgets and cash flow projections; critical audit-proofing tools
- Chart the events that led to the start of the business, and claim expenses from that point on
- Formalize all bookkeeping from Day 1. Open a separate bank account
- Classify all expenditures into their proper definition: operating or capital costs
- Expect to be audited, particularly if you are claiming tax losses over a period of years.

REAL LIFE: Marlen Macleod loved to cook. Over the years she had invented a number of taste-bud tempting new creations, but a few stood out as memorable to her family and friends. There was the tomato aspic that was special at Thanksgiving, the miniature chocolate sculptures on her cream puffs at Christmas time and her crown roast of pork barbecqued exquisitely for her mother's birthday bash, every August. In fact, after one particularly sumptuous girth-enhancing session, Marlen's friends remarked, "You know, you should really go into business!"

This common scene, played out daily in countless homes and workplaces throughout Canada often initiates entrepreneurship in those with both a product (or service) and vision. Yet, the flame of a small business owner's inspiration can quickly be doused if steps are not taken to shelter a fledgling enterprise from the gusts of Revenue Canada's audit department.

Marlen went on to become the town caterer and is today making plans to franchise her methods nationwide. However, she almost lost it all, when a tax auditor refused to see the potential in her and her start-up venture.

THE PROBLEM

Just when does a passion or a hobby become a viable business with a reasonable expectation of profit? The Income Tax Act provides limited guidance. It defines a business as follows:

> "A business includes a profession, calling, trade, manufacture or undertaking *of any kind whatever*. . .(including) an adventure or concern in the nature of trade, but does not include an office or employment."

This means that if you can make a profit from activities as diverse as gardening, walking your neighbours' dogs while they are on holidays, drawing ads or finding mates for the lovelorn, Revenue Canada will be obliged to agree that you are in fact in business. Unfortunately, the nature of business start-ups is usually that you must spend both time and money before you reap the rewards. The risk hopefully will justify the rewards, which often are several years away.

In the meantime, Revenue Canada's auditors have a window of time in which to probe your affairs and make a judgement call. This is usually the current tax year and up to two years back. The bad news? Revenue Canada can choose to put the blinders on and take a narrow view of your business results to date. In fact, if you are writing off business losses resulting from legitimate deductions that are fully documented, an auditor can take a hard-nosed view. . .that your intent is simply to take the expenses of a hobby, create a business loss and write it off to recover refunds of tax prepaid on other employment, pension or investment income.

THE SOLUTION

Start-up ventures can be a challenge for a Revenue Canada auditor and taxpayer alike. It's difficult, for example, not to get a little emotional, when you've struggled to keep your enterprise afloat for a couple of years, only to find yourself nose to nose with an auditor who is inferring you are cunningly trying to avoid paying tax on the income from the day job that's keeping you all fed in the meantime. This can be particularly distressing if you've run into some unanticipated road blocks along the way. So to begin your new relationship with Revenue Canada, there are two things you need to understand up front:

Don't take it personally   Unfortunately there are those taxpayers who do try to bend the rules or cheat the tax system, and they are the very ones who validate the tax compliance activities at Revenue Canada. Tax auditing has its place in ensuring that small business in Canada competes on a level playing field; where honest taxpayers can rest assured that tax cheats aren't undercutting pricing. Your role in a tax audit is to provide the information required for the auditor to understand and agree that you have a viable business enterprise with a reasonable expectation of profit *in the future.* See it as an exercise in both communication and education, and approach this part of any audit with confidence. Remember, *it is usually the person with the most knowledge who is the most successful.* At this point, that's you, because no one knows your business and its future better than you do.

Know the rules and how to play the game   The day you decided to open your business is the day you stepped up to the plate to play ball with Revenue Canada. You're in the game, and it's more than just a pastime: you're in the big leagues now. Imagine for a moment a baseball player capable of hitting a home run. However, by not studying in advance the tendencies of the pitcher, he could easily strike out. Likewise, you could be heading for a lucrative dollar contract, but if you don't bother to know the tax rules, Revenue Canada could strike you out despite your skills, ability and work ethic. To that end, in the back of your mind in the pursuit of all of your business activities, you should be prepared to qualify that you are in fact, a pro.

THE PARAMETERS

Professionals — those who get paid to do what they love to do best — conduct themselves in a professional manner. When business is your calling, your professional conduct is under scrutiny by your clients, your employees, your suppliers, your competitors, and yes, even Revenue Canada. For this reason, a specific code of conduct is required, particularly when it comes to your tax-filing obligations.

Open a Separate Business Bank Account
Never co-mingle personal and business funds. Also, obtain a separate charge card for the business. Never put business charges on your personal charge cards.

Business Start Criteria

In order for any amount to be deductible on the return, the taxpayer must be found to be "carrying on business" in the fiscal period in which the expense was incurred. So when are you considered to be in business? Did the expenses you incurred precede the start of the business, or did they take place after the business had commenced? When did the business actually start? Here are some guidelines, based on Revenue Canada's IT 364:

- A business starts whenever some significant activity that forms a regular part of the income-earning process takes place.
- There must be a specific concept of the type of business activity that will be carried on.
- An organizational structure must be in place to undertake the essential preliminaries, to show whether this is a one-time transaction, or an on-going enterprise.

The full utilization of start-up costs over the lifetime of your business is most important, as they can help you reduce profits in the future or reach back and gain access to past taxes paid. More on that later. Therefore, it is important not to lose this draw.

Following are some examples of activities that indicate whether or not business is considered by Revenue Canada to have started:

Figure 3.1   Revenue Canada's Considerations

Type of Activity	A Business Start?
Purchase of materials for resale	Yes
Review of various business opportunities	No
Market surveys are undertaken to establish place or method of carrying on the business	Yes
Construction of a hotel has started, together with staff recruitment, training, advertising, purchase of supplies for bedrooms, restaurant, etc.	Yes
Overviewing preliminary plans and/or various sites to determine whether the hotel business was the right opportunity	No
Steps are taken to obtain a required regulatory licence in advance of business activities starting	Yes
Assurances were negotiated in advance of the commencement of business activities that suppliers would perform	Yes
Steps were taken to obtain a patent	No
Manufacture of the patented goods begins	Yes

Hobby vs. Business

After determining a business start date, you'll have to convince Revenue Canada that you have a viable business that has a reasonable expectation of profit. This could be problematic in several areas, in which the taxman could take a hard line:

- The business is not making enough money to cover expenditures, and it looks doubtful it ever will
- The income from the business is not the chief source of income.

To be fair, many successful businesses start out as a hobby. . .something you enjoy and at which you perfect your skills, only to find it produces a business case sometime in the future. There are many such examples:

- The professor of music who writes in her spare time, touring with a local band of musicians to summer folk festivals to build up her name and image
- The photographer who is employed by a newspaper during the day and takes breath-taking wedding photographs on the weekend
- The mechanic who has invested thousands of dollars in his video and computer equipment in order to document the history of his passion — vintage vehicles — in what he hopes will be a best-selling coffee table book next Christmas
- The farmer who works in the city as a teacher by day, and raises his prize exotic poultry — geese, ducks and ostrich — when he comes home
- The housewife and mother of four who has turned her recipe for after-school nutritional "candy" into a Christmas fair bestseller.

The best way to prove that a business emerged and has a reasonable expectation of profit in the future is to keep a detailed record of all the activities that you have performed in the past to cross the line from activities pursued "for pleasure" to those pursued "for profit." You can do this best by keeping a *Daily Business Journal* (see page 37). It also helps to show how close you are to landing the deals you need to make yours a profitable venture.

Establish Your Business Start and Your Fiscal Year End

Unincorporated small businesses must end their fiscal period for reporting business income and deductions at December 31. An election may be made to select an off-calendar year end in specific cases — when there is a bona fide business reason to postpone the business year end. This could happen in the case of a retail outlet, which experiences its largest sales of the year in the month of December. (See *The Complete Canadian Home Business Guide to Taxes* by Evelyn Jacks for details.) Corporations may choose any 12-month period in which to end their fiscal reporting period. This could be June 1 to May 31; February 1 to January 31, and so on.

Set up Your Tax-Filing Framework.

For most businesses, there is a specific "framework" from which to work in approaching tax-filing obligations. This boils down to six easy parameters:

- **Methods of Reporting Income.** There are two methods of reporting income:
  - **The cash method:** Income is reported for tax purposes when it is actually received, and expenses are deducted when they are actually paid. This method is usually only available to farmers and very small businesses.
  - **The accrual method:** Most businesses must use the accrual method of accounting. Income is reported when "earned" (rather than received) and expenses are deducted as they are "incurred" (rather than actually paid). Professionals, like doctors and dentists, may report on a modified accrual basis, to take into account "work-in-progress," while other businesses may take special reserves in certain instances. (See *The Complete Canadian Home Business Guide to Taxes* by Evelyn Jacks for more details.)
- **Deduction of Operating Expenses.** Operating expenses are also known as "business inputs" in GST jargon; or those expenditures that are necessary for you to produce the goods and services that bring in the revenues. These are items that are "used up," like supplies, advertising and promotions, rent, salary, communications costs, licences, etc. These items are usually 100% deductible in the fiscal year in which they occurred, unless there are specific restrictions in place. When gross revenues earned are reduced by operating expenses the result may be either net operating loss or an operating profit.
- **Computation of Capital Cost Allowances.** When you acquire an asset with a useful life of more than one year, you must classify that asset into prescribed classes set out in the Income Tax Act. Prescribed rates of depreciation are claimed for those assets and the result is a deduction for Capital Cost Allowance or CCA. This subject is discussed in more detail later. However, the key concept here is that you don't want to make the mistake of taking a 100% deduction for an expenditure that Revenue Canada is going to reclassify as a capital one. That can lead to expensive surprises later.

It is also necessary to keep track of asset values on acquisition and disposition, whether or not a GST/HST rebate or input tax credit was received, an Investment Tax Credit was claimed, or a special accelerated rate is available.

The CCA claim also provides a series of tax-planning opportunities. For example, if operating expenses have already exceeded the gross revenues, it may be wise not to take the CCA deduction in the current year and "save" a higher undepreciated balance for use in the future. On the other hand, if the CCA deduction helps to increase or create a business loss that can be carried back to recover taxes paid in the prior three years, the taxpayer may wish to maximize the claim. Ask your tax advisor about this.

In addition, by reducing net business income with CCA, you may be able to save money on your CPP liability come April 30. This is significant for businesses in which net profit is about $37,000 or less.

- **Computation of Auto Expenses.** One of the most common deductions of the home-based business owner, these expenses are usually computed on a separate worksheet. The reason for this is so that you can first total all operating expenses like gas and oil, and all fixed expenses like interest on your car loan, and then prorate them according to the business driving you did during the year. It's necessary to have an auto log that reports both business and personal driving in order for you to come up with the deductibility ratio. Details are discussed in Chapter 6. Note that certain expenses can be claimed on an unreceipted basis: coin parking, car washes, pay telephones or any other expenses incurred where it is not possible to receive a receipt. Keep a log of such expenditures.

- **Computation of Home Workspace Costs.** Most home-based business owners will also be writing off home workspace costs, which is legitimate only if you have a separate area exclusively set aside for the business and if you regularly see clients or conduct your business from there. This is also computed on a separate worksheet in order to properly accomplish the proration of all total expenses of the home, including utilities, interest, insurance, property taxes, etc. As well, there is a special restriction to be aware of: home workspace expenses may not be used to create or increase an operating loss. When this happens, the balance of the home workspace expenses must be carried forward for use in future years when there is an operating profit.

- **Personal Use Allocation.** Most home-based business owners spend many long hours trying to get their businesses off the ground and use all the resources available to them to do so. This includes their own home, car, and other supplies, including the human resources inherent in available family members to get things off the ground. Many people make the mistake of underclaiming expenses that have a legitimate business component. We'll take a closer look at how to legitimize business-use components of specific expenses in Chapter 9.

To be sure, the Income Tax Act is very specific about personal or living expenses of the taxpayer. . .they may not be deducted, as per Section 18 (1)(h), other than travel expenses incurred by the taxpayer while away from home in the course of carrying on a business.

Personal and living expenses are specifically defined in the Act in Section 248. They include the expenses of the personal property, costs of a life insurance policy or expenses of properties that are maintained by a trust.

However, what you need to know is that so long as you make proper allowances for any personal component of an expense, the business portion of the expenses should be tax deductible, provided that the expenses are connected to the earning of income from the business.

If you're in the business of selling cosmetics, for example, you might write off all the expenses of make-up and skin care products that are used for resale. But if you fail to add back into income a reasonable amount for personal consumption, you can expect trouble from Revenue Canada's auditors, unless you can prove you never use any of the products yourself.

In another example, a masonry contractor, who ships a portion of interlocking bricks to his new home, and a portion to his client's worksite, would need to allocate the personal use portion of the expenses, or write off only the portion of the expense that pertained to his client.

Similar adjustments must be made by those who run clothing stores, grocery stores, farms, fishing enterprises and the like. In addition, costs of using capital assets that have both a personal and business usage — example, a car or your home office — must reflect reductions for personal use. Expect to be asked for the personal use allocation during an audit.

Meeting the Onus of Proof

For any expense to be deductible a couple of factors have to be in place:
- You have to meet an Onus of Proof, to show the amounts were actually incurred and are reasonable
- You have to incur the expense in order to produce income from your business.

Usually, you are considered innocent until proven guilty. However, compliance under the Income Tax Act has a slightly different twist:

Revenue Canada doesn't have to accept your return as filed. Rather, you have the obligation to prove that every figure on that return was correct and legitimate. There are two sections of the Income Tax Act to look to for guidance here:

- Section 67, which introduces the requirement for "reasonableness":

  "In computing income, no deduction shall be made in respect of an outlay or expense. . .except to the extent that (it) was reasonable in the circumstance."

- Section 18, which zeros in on the concept of "intent":

  "In computing the income of a taxpayer from a business or property, no deduction shall be made in respect of an outlay or expense except if it was incurred by the taxpayer for the purpose of gaining or producing income from the business or property."

To support your case for "reasonableness" you have to do two things:

- Keep meticulous records of all income and expenditures, including auto logs
- Keep your personal and business affairs completely separate.

In addition, the auditor must consider the following: gross income, net income, capital investment, cash flow, personal involvement, experience and training, plans for future development, and all other relevant factors which will be used to determine whether business income is taxable, and consequently whether any losses will be deductible in full or in part.

When it comes to recordkeeping, it matters not how sophisticated your computer system and software is. The finest reports will not bypass Revenue Canada's requirement for hard copy or microfilming. Guidelines for proper electronic imaging must be met, and can be obtained by calling the Canadian General Standards Board 1-800-665-2472.

You will be required to produce records, in an organized and readable manner, including:

- Accounts
- Agreements
- Books
- Charts
- Tables
- Diagrams
- Forms
- Images
- Invoices
- Letters
- Maps
- Memoranda
- Optical Disks
- Plans
- Returns
- Source Documents*
- Statements
- Telegrams
- Vouchers
- Any other thing that contains information, whether in writing or any other form.

* Source documents include sales invoices, purchase invoices, cash register receipts, formal written contracts, credit card receipts, delivery slips, deposit slips, work orders, dockets, cheques, bank statements, tax returns and general correspondence, according to Information Circular 78-10R3.

It is also necessary to keep an automobile distance log.

Record Retention

Your records must be kept at your place of business or your residence, and must be available to Revenue Canada auditors at reasonable times. Revenue Canada may reassess your tax returns at any time up to three years after the date on the original Notice of Assessment. If at any time fraud is suspected, however, the department can go as far back in your records as it wants, subject only to the record retention period. That is, you are only required to keep books and records until six years from the end of the last taxation year in which the records and books relate. You can request permission to destroy your records earlier than that, using Form T137; however, this may be an invitation for a tax audit first.

Know the Value of Your Tax Losses

When your total business expenditures exceed your income for the year, the resulting non-capital loss can be used to offset all other income of the year. If there is an excess loss, the remaining balance can be carried back for up to three years, or carried forward for up to seven years (ten years in the case of farmers).

So let's say that last year your income was $75,000. This year after losing your job, you start a business and incur a $10,000 non-capital loss. What's the value of that loss if you carry it back and offset last year's income? Well, at a 50% tax bracket, that's $5,000. . .which can go a long way to financing continual growth in your business. You see, you've just found some new money with your new-found tax knowledge.

But this is exactly the type of situation that can raise the flags in Revenue Canada's audit department, especially if you've been claiming these losses over a number of years. You'll need to be prepared to prove that the expenses were both reasonable and incurred to earn income, from a business with a reasonable expectation of profit.

THE TAX ADVISOR

The following action items will be necessary to start your business venture. Do them on your own or together with your tax advisors.

Register Your Business

When enough activities have commenced to indicate a business start, open a separate bank account for your business. Your next stop should be to your tax accountant and/or lawyer who will help you with the following:

- Whether or not to incorporate
- Whether to obtain a Business Number, required if it is advantageous or necessary to collect and remit GST/HST and/or to make payroll remittances on behalf of employees
- When to make payroll, GST/HST and PST remittances to avoid late-filing penalties
- When tax instalment payments are necessary
- Whether to register business names, trademarks and copyrights
- Whether provincial sales tax collections and remittances will be necessary
- Whether family assets need further protection
- Whether life insurance, disability and medical insurance should be obtained
- How your estate planning will be affected by the start-up venture
- Parameters in writing contracts with others
- How to protect yourself and your family from lawsuits by others.

Write Your Business Start Plan

The checklist on page 36 in Figure 3.2 should be consulted throughout the year to help you make major business start-up decisions.

By covering off the items in this Business Start Plan with your advisors, you will have most of the information a tax auditor will need to recognize you have taken steps not only to start a business formally, or to turn a hobby into a business, but also that there is a reasonable expectation of profit from your venture.

Start a Daily Business Journal

As you can tell by our previous discussions, even the commencement date of a business can be a debated matter when it comes to a tax audit. The best defense for the business owner to clinch the process, is to begin journalizing any and all activities that relate to the business as soon as possible. This can take any format you are comfortable with, but the key is to make notes of following points on page 37:

Figure 3.2	Your Business Start Plan	
Circumstance	**Decision**	**Action Plan**
Business Starts	Formalize Tax Position	- Prepare Business Plan: 1,3, 5 Years - Prepare annual budget - Prepare Cash Flow Journal - Start Daily Business Events Journal - Register business name/trademarks - Obtain Business Number - Open separate bank account - Consult professional advisors - Start recordkeeping system
Obtain Assets Used in Business	Buy, Lease or Convert existing assets to business use.	- Obtain Fair Market Value of car, home computer, other assets to be used in business. - Establish business location - Separate home workspace area - Obtain estimates on buying new or used - Obtain estimates on leasing options
Operating Expenses Commence	How Will Expenses Be Paid?	- Obtain Line of Credit or make equity contribution - Arrange terms from suppliers - Get business cards printed - Get letterhead printed - Establish separate business phone lines - Establish fax/e-mail communications - Prepare marketing materials
Plan Owner-Manager Compensation	How Will I Be Paid?	- Draw of Net Profits of Proprietorship, remuneration at FMV - Corporation: salary, bonus, dividends or shareholders loan?
Plan Income Splitting with Family Members	How Will I Pay Income to my Spouse or Children?	- Establish job descriptions - Write employment contracts - Begin source remittances
Enhance Family Lifestyle	How Can I Utilize Company-Paid Benefits?	- Company Pension Plans - Company Group Health Plans - RRSP contributions - Taxable/tax-free perks
Establish Operating Procedures	How Can I Expand?	- Document Policies and Procedures - Establish Organizational Structure - Prepare Marketing Plans - Prepare Development Plans - Prepare Product Distribution Plans - Prepare Quality Control Procedures - Prepare Follow-up Procedures - Prepare Client Relationship Procedures
Plan Equity Accumulation	How Will I be Paid Out?	- Establish family succession plans - Plan for tax-free capital gains - Establish current valuation of business - Set a price. . .you never know when an offer may come along
Plan for Your Demise	What Taxes Will Be Payable?	- Anticipate deemed disposition rules - Ensure life insurance will cover taxes

- Every phone call made to do research, enquire about how to find a supplier, get a business licence, lease a location, buy a computer, etc.
- Every networking appointment. Keep all business cards from potential customers, suppliers, or others who will be associated with you in your business
- Every lead in bringing you to the next step in your business development
- Every hour worked on the project
- All distances driven in pursuit of your business activities.

A sample format follows in Figure 3.3.

This Daily Business Journal can be your key to tax audit survival. It shows intent and reasonableness at the same time.

Figure 3.3	Daily Business Journal

Date:

Time	To Do	Incoming Items	Follow-up	Expense Details
6:00 a.m.	Breakfast			km: 36,544
7:00	e-mail		Meet L. Jones	
8:00	Meeting T. Cook		Prepare Quote	Coffee $5.00
9:00	Prepare Market Plan			
10:00	"			
11:00	Mail/Telephone Calls	See log attached		
12:00 p.m.	Meet Banker @ Tini's			Lunch $35.00 km 36,660 B
1:00				
2:00	L. Jones @ Earl's		Prepare Quote	Coffee $5.00 km 36,670 B
3:00	Market Plan			
4:00	Meet Printer @ shop		Proof designs	km 36,750 B
5:00	Exercise			km 36,780 P
6:00	Supper			km 36,800 P
7:00	Finish Market plan			
8:00	e-mail			
9:00	Family time			

Total Expenses: $45.00   **Total Travel: 256 km**   **Business Travel: 206 km**

Keep it faithfully and dig it out should the taxman visit your enterprise. It is the story of your business's past, present and future; a crucial element in *"making sure it's deductible!"*

Formalize Your Books and Keep All Receipts

If you're a hopeless bookkeeper, do yourself and Revenue Canada a favour by hiring someone to do this job for you, at least monthly. You simply can't afford not to. You'll be busy starting up the business, recruiting the staff, finding the income to cover the costs and managing the distribution of your goods and services. You'll also be responsible for keeping your Daily Business Journal, which is a critical tool in ensuring that your expenditures are deductible during a tax audit. Poor recordkeeping can stall your business, so put this into place. Here's the minimum reporting structure you want to see to keep on top of your business activities:

Figure 3.4	Required Reports		
Daily	**Weekly Totals**	**Monthly**	**Quarterly**
Bank Deposits	Bank Deposits	Income Statement	Income Statement
Dollar volume	Dollar volume	Balance Sheet	Balance Sheet
Units Sold	Units Sold	Sales Statistics	Sales Statistics
Staff hours	Staff hours	Marketing Statistics	Marketing Statistics
	NSF Cheque Records	Payroll Remittances	GST/HST Reporting
	Accounts Payable	Cash Flow Requirements	

It's important to keep these records right from the start. They will provide you with an ability to compare next year's results with your start-up year, and to budget for and chart the growth of your business.

Write It Off, Write It All Off

Look upon every expenditure you make in terms of its potential for reducing your taxes, and keep all the hard copy: receipts, invoices, etc. (see Chapter 9).

Keep Track of Your Automobile Costs and Business Driving

Start an Auto Log immediately. Record all expenses of operating the vehicle, the fair market value of the vehicle at the time you started using it for business activities, and the distance you drive with that car: both personal and business kilometres must be kept, faithfully, to help you claim your auto expenses on your return. A sample format follows:

Figure 3.5	Auto Log

Date	km Start	km Finish	Destination	Reason for trip	Gas/Oil	M & R	Wash	Park	Other

Plan How to Take Your Tax-Efficient Profits

While Revenue Canada concentrates on catching the tax cheats, you should now have that part of your tax house in order with the set-up of procedures that allow for full compliance. With those basics out of the way, you can concentrate on setting up your affairs to make and report your profits in the most tax-efficient manner. That's where you should be spending the time and money with your advisors in the first place. Remember the reason why you are in business: to make profits and build equity over the long run to your best advantage. Below are a few basics on maximizing after-tax profits.

Figure 3.6	Taxation of Income of a Business Owner

TYPES OF BUSINESS ORGANIZATIONS

Unincorporated Proprietor	**Incorporated Business**	**Partnership**
Taxed on Net Profits of the Business; not salary or draws	- Taxed as employee - Taxed on certain benefits - Taxed on dividends received as a shareholder - Taxed on sale of equity	Whether incorporated or not, the profits are split and allocated to partners based on details of the partnership agreement.

A Proprietor Can Reduce Taxable Income by:

- Making maximum RRSP contributions
- Minimizing instalment payments, interest, and penalities
- Reducing net business income with CCA deductions, paying operational expenses before year end, buying capital assets before year end, keeping auto log books to maximize car expenses, paying family members to split income and create RRSP room for them
- Deferring income into the future with timing of contracts, if that otherwise makes good business sense.

An Incorporated Business Owner May Reduce Taxable Income Personally by:

- Setting the level of employment income to minimize source deductions, which affect the cash flow needed by the business. Suggestion: a maximum of $75,000 annually to maximize RRSP Room. Other possible threshholds: $29,590 keeps you in the lowest tax bracket; $59,180 keeps you out of the top tax bracket. Taxpayers who make $6,956 in 1999 pay no personal taxes.
- Set bonus payments when the corporation makes a profit. These payments might be taken over two tax years to minimize personal tax. Or, you can decide to pay the bonuses to your family members who work with you, if by doing so you minimize the family tax liability.
- Set dividend payments. Make these throughout the year if you need the money; but consider making at least one in January of the next tax year. You won't have to pay source deductions in advance through the company, and you'll have use of the money for a full 16 months more: January 1, 1999, to April 30, 2000, for example.
- Consider paying taxable and tax-free benefits to yourself and family members. (This will be discussed in more detail in Chapter 8.)
- Interest on shareholders loans: If you own your own corporation, it is possible for you to take a shareholder's loan. Under general rules, if this amount is not repaid within one year of the end of the tax year in which it was made, the amounts are added to your income. However, changes announced by the Department of Finance in April 1995 will allow loans made to shareholders who are also employees to be considered exempt from income inclusion if the loans were made because of the employment conditions (i.e., a loan to acquire a company car), and bona fide repayments were arranged.

Make sure you speak with your tax advisor about structuring compensation packages to take advantage of as many of these perks as possible.

RECAP: 10 Simple Steps to Starting a Tax-Efficient Small Business

1. **Acknowledge your new relationship with Revenue Canada**. Make a point of understanding your obligations to report income under the law, keep records, make remittances like instalments,

source deductions, and GST/HST. Be prepared to open your books to Revenue Canada's audit scrutiny.

2. **Always document and separate personal-use components of any of your expenditures**, and open separate business bank and charge card accounts.

3. **Know when your business is considered to have started**. When did it go from being a sideline or hobby to a viable going concern? The key is. . .when was there a reasonable expectation of profit or earning income from the business?

4. **Establish your fiscal year end.** This is normally December 31 for most unincorporated small business organizations; however, speak to your tax advisor if you feel there is a bona fide business reason to choose a non-calendar year end.

5. **Write a formal business start plan**, including a marketing and cash flow analysis plan, a formal budget and set up the ability to make comparative reports in the future. These documents will all go a long way to winning a tax audit.

6. **Start keeping a Daily Business Journal** to document your networking, contacts with suppliers and others who will help you build and grow your business. Keep your auto distance travel logs in here as well.

7. **Classify deductible expenditures properly**, into operational and capital items, to facilitate proper applications and do some long-term tax planning.

8. **Know the value of your tax losses** and how to apply them to other income in the current year and in the carry-over periods.

9. **Meet the Onus of Proof** — annually. The ability to defend the "grey areas" is a position of power you do not want to give up to a tax auditor, who doesn't know your business or your business plans as well as you do. You can show reasonable expectation of profit better than the auditor can. . .don't give up your edge by keeping poor records during the year.

10. **Review your business organization structure often**: at least every six months. Is the proprietorship the best format, or should you be considering a partnership or incorporation? Is there a better way to split income with family members or a better compensation structure for the owner-manager? Discuss these items with your advisors.

CHAPTER 4

Write Off More Deductions Without Changing Your Life

"You must first clearly see a thing in your mind before you can do it."
ALEX MORRISON

KEY CONCEPTS

- There are two problematic "grey areas" Revenue Canada can use to disallow your claims
  - One is used when the taxpayer writes off business losses against other income for too many years
  - The other occurs when Revenue Canada suspects your income is understated
- Deductibility of business expenses depends largely on whether there is a source of income now, or the potential for one in the future
- Expenses that were incurred in the process of earning income from the business are deductible, even if there is a "mixed use"; that is, some personal and some business component.

REAL LIFE: Julie was blessed with a special gift — the ability to express herself in painting beautiful Canadian landscapes for reprint on greeting cards. Her studio was in her home, from where she produced, marketed and distributed the cards nationwide. Her twin sister Janet was a writer, employed by the local paper. Her quick wit and quirky sense of humour landed her the role of feature freelance columnist — a job she enjoyed. She also wrote thoughtful messages for her sister's works, on a contract basis. With the pressure of writing a daily column, she often joined her sister Julie in the beautiful mountains of British Columbia, gaining inspiration and insight for their respective art forms.

The sisters, both earning income in the $75,000 range, found they were paying remarkably dissimilar amounts of tax. This prompted a visit to their tax advisor, who confirmed that both their returns had previously been pre-pared mathematically correctly — but not to their best overall benefit.

Janet, it appeared, was passive about claiming all the deductions she was entitled to. Julie, who knew more about her rights and obligations, fared better. Their advisor, however, found that they could both be dramatically decreasing the amount of taxes they were paying, without dramatically changing their lives. They needed to take a fresh look at the costs of run-ning their respective businesses, now and in the future, and redefine their obligations to the taxman.

However, like many Canadian taxpayers, the twins were afraid to appear too aggressive, because the last thing they needed was trouble with Rev-enue Canada!

THE PROBLEM

Every day Canadian business people are contemplating a variety of business transactions and asking *"Will it be Deductible?"* How does one intelligently make the judgement call? This can be a real concern for many taxpayers, and legitimately so.

That is because our Income Tax Act alone does not provide the guid-ance fully required to assess the way Canadians file their returns. There are, in addition, a number of filing policies enacted by Revenue Canada, and these policies, together with the law encoded in the Act itself, are prone to a variety of subjective interpretations by both sides.

What's more, the Income Tax Act grants to Revenue Canada a number of arbitrary powers. In fact, under Section 152(7), Revenue Canada has the right to change your tax return if they don't agree with the way you've filed it. They can change your income figures, your deductions or your credits prior to the expiration of your reassessment period, which is normally three years. Your tax-filing fate, therefore, can rest with an auditor who perceives your *tax and personal affairs* quite differently than you do. Given this reality, it's often very difficult to say in advance whether your business expense will ultimately be deductible or not.

For some, this is scary stuff. These grey areas of interpretation by two opposing parties could be seen to be somewhat weighted in favour of the taxman. . .sort of like playing ball against a team who knows more of the rules and also has all the referees on their side. Does the audit process itself lead to inequality in the ultimate tax assessment of two taxpayers with like enterprises and income levels? Do those who get audited, pay more tax than those who don't?

These are all legitimate questions. In a recent report, *Compliance: From Vision to Strategy*, Revenue Canada admitted that it is the complexity, particularly the "grey" areas in tax law and tax planning, that are the most problematic for taxpayers and tax auditors alike. This reality has given birth to many expensive court challenges.

The results of recent court challenges on the deductibility of expenses in a variety of different cases, clearly illustrate the nature of taxation for small business owners: they have often hinged on interpretation of individual facts, and on their individual tax-filing profile. For example:

Fuel for the Body

In a 1998 appeal to the Tax Court (Scott, 98 DTC 6530), a taxpayer who was a self-employed foot and public transit courier, tried to claim the daily cost of food and water needed to keep up the pace of his work during the day. The Tax Court dismissed his case, stating they found those expenses to be personal in nature. The Federal Court of Appeal disagreed. While food and beverages consumed during a work day are normally considered to be a personal expense, the court found that in this case, the courier had to eat and drink more than normal; in fact, if fuel for an auto was deductible, so should fuel for the body be. The result? A reasonable amount of the expenses should be allowed as a tax deduction.

Sufficient Start-up Time

In a case involving a rental property (Gideon, 98 DTC 1788), a doctor and her husband acquired a rental property that suffered losses when adverse economic factors were encountered. Despite the fact that they charged rent proven to be reasonable, reduced the mortgage quickly to minimize interest payments and that the size of the rental losses were steadily decreasing over time, Revenue Canada took a hard-line position and reassessed the couple's tax returns to disallow the rental losses claimed over a period of three years. The Federal Court of Appeal allowed the appeal and scolded Revenue Canada for failing to allow the taxpayers a sufficient start-up time in which to make a profit. Given the way in which the taxpayers conducted this venture, it appeared to the judge that there was a reasonable expectation of profit in the future.

Home Sales Produced Profits, Not Capital Gains

Failure to recognize a profitable business can bring dismal tax news. This is exactly what happened when a taxpayer built a series of houses and resold each of them in a short period of time (Mullin, 98, DTC 1731). A number of these homes were built in a subdivision owned by the taxpayer's father. In this case, one house was allowed as a tax-exempt principal residence, as the taxpayer and his wife lived in the home. However, the taxpayer had not been able to convince the Judge that the other homes were built for investment purposes, because of the "quick flip" in sales. As a result, 100% of the profits from those sales were included in income.

The Dentist and His Sheep

Revenue Canada restricted the farming losses of a dentist who raised cattle for five years and then decided to raise sheep. The good doctor was able to beat the taxman by showing he had spent 60 hours or more each week in pursuit of his farming activities, while he practised dentistry less than 24 hours per week. He was also able to show that his investment in the farm was substantial and that over the years, his chief source of income had changed: now it was from the farming operation (Langtot, 98, DTC 1475).

Credibility Wins Over the Judge

The commission sales agent faced the wrath of the taxman when his records and log books were, well, skimpy. The Judge at the Tax Court of Canada, found him to be totally credible and allowed him to claim expenses as a deduction as a result. The Model Citizen Factor pays off again (Rusnak, 98, DTC 1271).

These cases reinforce what you learned in the last chapter on setting foundations for business start-ups: because you have the ability to tell the story of your business circumstances; your intent now and in the future, your activities in pursuit of future profits, you likely have the components for a successful case. In fact, for some, a tax audit can actually be a profitable experience (see Chapter 10).

THE SOLUTION

If you want to make sure your expenditures are tax deductible, you must remember the other side of the deductibility equation: that the business owner must prove there is a reasonable expectation of *profit* from the business venture. That is to say, there must be a source of income or a potential for that source sometime in the *foreseeable future*. Many taxpayers and their advisors underdevelop this argument during an appeals process, and lose their case.

This shouldn't be, as no one knows *the potential for future profits* of your business better than you do. The auditor can only make a judgement call on what *is* and what *was* in the reassessment period. You can paint the vision of the potential for income in the future, which is your right and privilege under the Income Tax Act:

"No deduction shall be made in respect of an outlay or expense except to the extent that it was made or incurred by the taxpayer *for the purpose of gaining or producing income from the business. . ."*

ITA Section 18(1) (a)

"It is not necessary to show that income actually resulted from the particular outlay or expenditure itself. It is sufficient that the outlay or expense was a *part of the income-earning process."*

Revenue Canada's Interpretation Bulletin IT 487

"An expense would not be disallowed simply because the income-earning process produced a loss, as long as *the intention* in making the expenditure was to produce income." Outlays or expenses made or incurred *to maintain income* or *to reduce other expenses* are also deductible as their purpose would be to increase income, whether or not such an increase resulted."

IT 487

THE PARAMETERS

There are only three key concepts you must fully understand in order to make the judgement calls about the deductibility of your expenditures, assuming they are reasonable:

- The outlay must be part of an income-earning process, in a business carried on for profit, or with a reasonable expectation of profit.
- There must be an intention to produce income, maintain income or reduce other expenses.
- Expenses claimed must not be personal or living expenses of the taxpayer.

Following are several parameters you must follow in specific business circumstances to come out ahead with the tax auditor on the issue of reasonable expectation of profit.

THE INCOME-EARNING PROCESS

An element of reasonableness must be present within your business enterprise. For example, imagine a writer who publishes one article a month, at a rate of $100 per article. His $1,200 of income a year is not enough to offset the cost of office supplies, home office expenses, courier costs, and so on. Should this person be allowed to write off losses against other income sources? That will depend on whether it can be shown that a reasonable expectation of future profits exists. In this case, the taxpayer will have to show what activities have taken place to increase the revenues from this business. Perhaps he's also written a book or a screenplay and is currently negotiating its rights, for example.

Field Code Matching

You'll note that field codes are given to certain figures on the Business Activities Statement that Revenue Canada wants to match and analyze (see sample on page 50). The first is Net sales on Line 8000, which is the total of sales, commissions or other fees earned in your business, net of federal or provincial sales taxes and any returns, allowances or discounts that were included in the gross sales figure. These categories should be discussed with your bookkeeper, who should set up the following accounts:

- Gross Sales (which you can break out into types of sales), before taxes
- GST/HST collected
- Provincial sales taxes collected
- Returns of sold items
- Allowances on sold items
- Discounts included in Gross Sales.

Also set up an account for Other Income sources that are outside the normal sales venues on Line 8230.

Cost of Goods Sold

Those who stock inventory will have to keep meticulous track of opening inventory, purchases, cost of sub-contracting and direct wage costs in producing the inventory. From all of these items the closing inventory value is subtracted to arrive at Cost of Goods Sold. You'll notice that only the business portion of costs are to be included here. This is particularly important for direct sellers in the cleaning, jewelry and other home sales enterprises. Those who use any part of their purchases for personal consumption — grocery items, cleaning supplies, jewelry worn personally, clothing worn personally, etc. — must account for this. You may not write off the costs of any inventory items that are used personally. Make sure you keep a separate log to identify such items and their value and be prepared to show this in a tax audit. In that way the auditor can see you have accounted for personal use, and will be less likely to rule "no reasonable expectation of profit."

Gross Profit (Line 8519)

This is a very important point of analysis for Revenue Canada. For example, let's say your net sales on Line 8000 were $25,000 during the year, but after computing Cost of Goods Sold, gross profit is only $5,000. From this all your other expenses of running the operation — from marketing costs to professional fees and wage costs — all must be paid. You find yourself in the hole by $15,000, on Line 9369 Net income (loss) before adjustments.

Margin Analysis

A close look at line 8000 Sales and Line 8519 tells the story of profit margins in your enterprise. If your retail pricing to the customer is not high enough to cover your operating expenses, your tax auditor has the right to say there is no reasonable expectation of profit. Fact is, you'll always be in a loss position at Line 9369, even if all your operating expenses are legitimate and documented. Most serious business people would want to reassess time and efforts closely to decide whether or not to continue in the same vein, given those poor showings. Change is necessary to stay afloat. *So, Step 1 in making sure your expenditures are deductible, and resulting operational losses can be used to offset other income of the year, is to plan for reasonable profit margins now or in the future.*

Attention to Source of Income

When Revenue Canada rules no reasonable expectation of profit, and thereby disallows your business losses, there are a couple of issues to address:

• Is this a personal endeavour? Why or why not?
• Will this endeavour result in profits in the future? Why?

To answer the first question, you can rely on Section 248, which describes a "business" to include "a profession, calling, trade, manufacture or *undertaking of any kind whatever..."* This should be bolstered with a listing of activities that would normally fall outside of the definition of a hobby, which is defined by Webster's Dictionary as "something a person likes to do or study in his spare time; a favourite pastime or a vocation." You will need to show that your undertaking goes far beyond a pastime or something you do in your spare time.

To answer the second question you'll need to produce your business plans, including marketing plans, networking activities and other indicators of pursuit of profit. Without the potential for a source of income, Reveneu Canada is within its rights to disallow your expenses.

Sample 4.1 Statement of Business Activities

Revenue Revenu
Canada Canada

STATEMENT OF BUSINESS ACTIVITIES

T2124-A
(97)

- For more information on how to complete this statement, see the income tax guide called *Business and Professional Income*.

2

Identification

Your name	Your social insurance number

For the period from:	YYYY MM DD 1998/01/01	to:	YYYY MM DD 1998/12/31	Was 1998 the final year of business?	Yes ☐	No ☒

Name of business	Main product or service

Business address	Industry code (see the appendix in the *Business and Professional Income* guide)

City, town or municipality, and province	Postal code	Partnership identification number

Name and address of person or firm preparing this form	Tax shelter identification number

Business number	Your percentage of the partnership	%

Income

Sales, commissions, or fees		(a)
Minus- GST and PST or HST (if included in sales above)		
- Returns, allowances, and discounts (if included in sales above)		
Total of the above two lines		(b)
Net sales, commissions, or fees (line a minus line b)	8000	
Reserves deducted last year	8290	
Other income	8230	
Gross income (total of the above lines) enter on the appropriate line of your income tax return	8299	(c)

Calculation of cost of goods sold (enter business portion only)

Opening inventory (include raw materials, goods in process, and finished goods)	8300	
Purchases during the year (net of returns, allowances, and discounts)	8320	
Sub-contracts	8360	
Direct wage costs	8340	
Other costs	8450	
Total of the above five lines		
Minus - Closing inventory (include raw materials, goods in process, and finished goods)	8500	
Cost of goods sold	8518	(d)
Gross profit (line c minus line d)	8519	(e)

Expenses (enter business portion only)

Advertising	8521	
Bad debts	8590	
Business tax, fees, licences, dues, memberships, and subscriptions	8760	
Delivery, freight, and express	9275	
Fuel costs (except for motor vehicles)	9224	
Insurance	8690	
Interest	8710	
Maintenance and repairs	8960	
Management and administration fees	8871	
Meals and entertainment (allowable portion only)	8523	
Staff meal and entertainment expenses after Feb. 23, 1998		
Motor vehicle expenses	9281	
Office expenses	8810	
Supplies	8811	
Legal, accounting, and other professional fees	8860	
Property taxes	9180	
Rent	8910	
Salaries, wages, and benefits (including employer's contributions)	9060	
Travel	9200	
Telephone and utilities	9220	
Private health services plan premiums (family)		
Other expenses	9270	
Capital cost allowance (from Area A on page 3 of this form)	9936	
Allowance on eligible capital property	9935	
Total business expenses (total of the above three lines)	9368	(f)
Net income (loss) before adjustments (line e minus line f)	9369	

Page 1

Courtesy of CANTAX Tax Preparation Software.

Business Expenses Only

You'll notice that the Statement of Business Activities calls for the business portion of expenses only. All expenditures of the business must be prorated if there is any personal use component. This is where many taxpayers really miss out on legitimate deductions, and some suggestions on maximizing these items follow in the Tax Advisor section.

As you now know, the trick to claiming audit-proof operational expenses is for a reasonable expectation of profit to be present at Line 8519. After this, *adequate documentation is the key,* as you'll need to produce receipts for the amounts claimed on Lines 8521 to 9935, and to be able to show they are reasonable in relation to income expected to be earned in the future. Always document why you made the expenditure in the first place. If you can, get into the habit of writing a note on the back of the receipt or invoice:

• Lunch, James Cook, re quote on supplies
• Gift, L. Smith, re thanks for contract
• Dinner, T. Tromblin, re rental property
• Flyers re Maryville campaign.

Reasonable operational expenses are generally 100% deductible in the year they are incurred. For guidance, you might look to Revenue Canada's Interpretation Bulletins, which are not necessarily binding in every case, but they can go a long way in helping you anticipate Revenue Canada's position on a matter, particularly at the Notice of Objection stage, and to helping you make your case on the basis of reasonableness. Following are interpretations regarding commonly deducted operational expenses:

Accounting and Legal Fees   The key pitfall taxpayers run into here is that they write off accounting and legal fees in full in cases where they really relate to capital transactions. Revenue Canada has issued IT-99R4 to address certain specific cases when legal or accounting fees will be deductible. They will be 100% deductible when paid in normal business activities like preparing contracts, collecting trade debts, preparing minutes of directors' meetings, conducting appeals for sales or property tax assessments and so on. They may even be deductible in defense of a charge of performance of illegal activities, depending on the relationship of the conduct to the income-earning activities. (Also see comments re Damages, on page 52.) Fees for preparing income tax returns and assistance in preparing an appeal on assessment of income taxes, interest or penalties, CPP or EI premiums will be deductible, as will the costs of preparing advance tax rulings.

However, when legal and accounting fees are incurred on the acquisition of capital property, they are normally included in the cost of the property, or as an outlay or expense in the case of dispositions of capital property.

Legal fees surrounding successful corporate acquisitions will be treated as capital expenses added to the cost base of the shares acquired. Legal and accounting fees incurred in an abortive attempt to acquire shares would normally not be deductible at all unless the taxpayer can demonstrate that s/he intended to make the business a part of a similar business already operated by the taxpayer.

Convention Expenses   This is a real problem area for taxpayers at audit time. First, self-employed taxpayers may claim the costs of *only two conventions* a year provided that they were held by a business or professional organization. While you need not be a member of the organization, you must have had an income-earning purpose related to your business in attending the convention. In addition, IT 131R2 explains another little-known requirement: that the convention be "held at a location that may reasonably be regarded as consistent with the territorial scope of the organization." An example of this would be an ocean cruise held by a Canadian organization. Therefore taxpayers must be cautioned to choose their convention locations wisely — as only two per year are deductible in the first place — and ensure they can prove that attending a convention in another country is directly related to their business or profession.

Damages and Settlements Paid   If you incur damages resulting from a normal risk of your business operations, a deduction for the costs, including interest payments or wrongful dismissal payments, will normally be allowed as fully deductible, unless the damages are on account of capital, in which case they would be classified as "eligible capital property." In such cases, three-quarters of the value of the damages are scheduled in the Cumulative Eligible Capital account, and may be deducted at a rate of 7% of that value per year.

Non-Competition Agreements   Here's a "dark horse" for any business owner who sells his or her company down the road and agrees to work under an employment contract that includes a non-competition clause. Any such payment received in exchange for the agreement not to compete can be classified as an "eligible capital expenditure" which means that only 75% of the amount will be subject to tax.

Hospitality

Revenue Canada has issued IT 518R to overview their position with regard to the deductibility of food, beverages and entertainment. Reasonable amounts may of course be deducted, if incurred to earn income from a business or property. The total costs must, however, be restricted to 50% of the amounts actually paid or payable. Note this 50% limitation will not apply to the computation of the personal tax liability on the T1 General in the following cases:

- The claiming of moving expenses using Form T1M
- The claiming of child care expenses using Form T778
- The claiming of medical expenses.

For details of claiming these amounts, please see *Jacks on Tax Savings* by Evelyn Jacks. However, it is important to know that the 50% limitation does apply to taxes and tips left as well as to restaurant gift certificates purchased as a gift for your client. The small business owner must be aware of several exceptions to the 50% restriction which will result in 100% claims on his/her Statement of Business Activities, as discussed below:

- **The Hospitality Business.** Costs of food, beverages or entertainment provided in the ordinary course of business, which is the business of providing food, beverages or entertainment to others in return for compensation. Restaurants, hotels and airlines, therefore, are all exempt from the 50% restriction on food, beverages or entertainment provided to their customers.
- **The Food & Beverage Business.** If the business you conduct is the business of making food, beverages or entertainment, cost of promotional samples is 100% deductible. However, any time you take someone out for a business meal, the costs will be subject to the 50% rules.
- **Registered Charities.** The 50% restriction will not apply if the food, beverages or entertainment are for a fund-raising event to primarily benefit a charity. The 50% rule will apply to the price of admission to an event that is part of the regular activities of the charity. For instance, Morena invites her client, Gustav, to the annual fund-raising dinner of the Manitoba Theatre for Young People. The expenses in that case are not subject to the 50% rules. Next week, she will be giving Gustav tickets to the groups five new plays to be held over the next seven months. The cost of those tickets are subject to the 50% rule.

- **Consultant's Billings.** If you do work for a company that entails travel or work "on location," and if the costs of meals are billed to the client and reimbursed to you, you are able to fully deduct those meal expenses, as the reimbursement would be included in your income.
- **Meals at Conferences.** Where an all-inclusive fee is paid, entitling the participant to food, beverages and/or entertainment, a $50 amount is allocated for each day to be the amount that's subject to the 50% restriction. All other costs will be fully deductible.
- **Beverages en Route.** You can fully deduct the cost of any meals and beverages served or entertainment provided on planes, trains or buses, so keep a log of those expenditures, as receipts are normally not available, and Revenue Canada will allow a reasonable amount as your claim.
- **Employer-Sponsored Events.** When you entertain your staff, you'll be able to avoid the 50% limitation on food, beverages and entertainment, provided that these are generally available to all employees at a particular place and enjoyed by them, like a Christmas party. After February 24, 1998, such events are limited to six per year.
- **Employer-Operated Restaurants or Cafeterias.** Costs of food, beverages here are not subject to the 50% rule, but subsidized meals do present a taxable benefit to the employees. Restricted facilities like an executive lounge or dining room are always subject to the 50% limitation.

Note that the following activities will qualify as entertainment subject to the 50% rules:

- Tickets to theatre, concerts, athletic events
- Private boxes at sporting events
- Cost of a cruise
- Admission to a fashion show
- Hospitality suites
- Entertaining at athletic or sporting clubs
- Entertaining while on vacation
- Cost of taxes, gratuities and cover charges
- Cost of security escorts
- Cost of escorts or tour guides*

* Costs of "escort services" are not deductible at all. So now you know.

Fines and Penalties

Taxpayers often want to know if they can write off parking tickets and speeding tickets incurred while in pursuit of business income. In general judicial and statutory fines and penalties are not deductible; however certain exceptions to the rules exist, according Revenue Canada's IT 104R2, if the following tests are met:

- The fine or penalty was laid out for the purpose of earning income
- Allowing the deduction would not be contrary to public policy
- Incurring the type of fine or penalty received is a normal risk of carrying on business, even though due care is exercised, and in general the violation is inevitable and beyond the control of the taxpayer and/or his/her employees
- The break does not result from negligence, ignorance or deliberate disobedience of the law and does not endanger the public
- It is not a capital outlay and not incurred to earn tax-exempt income.

What this tells us is that a courier may face the inevitability of receiving parking tickets in his/her job, which likely will be tax deductible. Revenue Canada clearly points out that pollution and speeding offenses will not be deductible under any circumstances.

Other notable non-deductible amounts are fines and penalties levied by professional organizations against their members.

Interest Costs

Interest costs on money borrowed at a reasonable rate of interest will generally be deductible as a business expense. Interest expenses will not be deductible in the following cases:

- The loan is interest free or the interest costs payable are not reasonable
- The money is not used directly in the pursuit of income from a business with a reasonable expectation of profit
- Income from property does not include capital gains accruals and therefore income in the form of dividends, rents or interest must be present for interest deductibility on loans used to acquire capital properties to be allowed.

Many business owners are unaware of the election to capitalize the cost of borrowed money used to acquire depreciable property. This election can be made for the current year and the three immediately preceding years, and for one, some or all of the properties acquired. It can also be made for all the money borrowed or some of it. An election under Section 21(1) or (3) of the Income Tax Act must be made and submitted with the tax return each year to opt for the treatment. Then the amount of the interest is simply added to the capital cost of the property and written off as part of the CCA claim each year. Look to Revenue Canada's IT 121R3 for more details.

Training Expenses

How much of your training costs — including travel, food, beverages and lodging paid to attend a training course — can you actually claim as a business deduction? There are several important rules to observe here, as outlined in IT 357R2:

New Skill or Upgrading?   Training costs will not be deductible if they are considered to be "capital" in nature; that is if they result in a lasting benefit to the taxpayer. This could include the acquisition of a new skill or qualification. However, if training is taken to maintain, update or upgrade an existing skill, the costs are 100% deductible. . .that is unless they are also being claimed as a non-refundable tax credit under the tuition fee amount.

Examples of expenses that are 100% deductible are:

- A professional development course taken to maintain professional standards
- A tax course taken by a lawyer or accountant, whether or not such work has been done previously
- A course on modern building materials is taken by an architect.

Therefore, training costs to attend a course which results in a degree, diploma, professional qualification or similar certificate is considered to be "capital" in nature. The costs would be scheduled in the Cumulative Eligible Capital account. Examples of this are the following:

- Training by a medical practitioner to qualify as a specialist
- Lawyer taking an engineering course unrelated to the legal practice
- A professor taking a sideline course to acquire skills in a sideline business.

Personal Portion   Any portion of the costs that are personal in nature cannot be deducted. This is assessed on a case-by-case basis and takes factors like duration and location of the course into account, as well as the number of days in which there was no training. It is also important that the costs not be misclassified. If they are really convention expenses, you could be restricted to the "two per year rule" and "territorial scope" rules identified earlier.

Location and Duration   Deductibility of expenses will be questioned if courses are taken abroad or in a resort, particularly if you follow up the course with a personal holiday. If equivalent training was available locally, your expenses for the trip to study at the exotic location will likely be considered personal. Costs for expenses of food and lodging will not be allowed for any days in which no training was held. Revenue Canada will make an exception for arrival and departure dates, as well as weekends, and allow those costs. Remember that the costs of claiming food and auto are subject to the normal limitations.

Deductibility of Seminars Are they classified as conventions or training courses? This is a question of fact. Conventions generally include a formal meeting of members of an organization or association. Training courses generally have a classroom format and a formal course of study that results in testing and possibility certification. Training courses are treated more favourably in that you can attend more than two in a year, however, Interpretation Bulletin 357R2 makes a noteworthy comment: the total time taken in attending courses in any one year must not be so great as to interfere with the carrying on of the taxpayer's business. If that happens, expenses will not be deductible.

Resources are Many, Varied and Often Free

In conclusion, if you are wondering about the deductibility of a specific classification of expenses, don't hesitate to find out from Revenue Canada whether an Interpretation Bulletin or other tax information is available. This will give you guidance on the position the department will likely be taking on the issue, and help you with the peace of mind issue.

Now you're ready to tackle the "grey areas." This refers to the special circumstances that make your business transactions fall outside the normal parameters outlined by Revenue Canada. There are a couple of things to remember, as you learned in Chapter 4, How to Start a Small Business. If you decide to take an aggressive stance and claim deductions for items that could be called into question, you want to make sure you have a bona fide business purpose documented for each expenditure, and that your business has a reasonable expectation of profiting from your activities and expenditures. The following may be of some help in audit-proofing those decisions.

TAX ADVISOR

To audit-proof your expenditures and help you *"Make Sure It's Deductible,"* you may wish to take advantage of some of the checklists below to help you make sound judgement calls that ensure your books are prepared in your favour:

Tax Deductibility Standard

Before spending the money, take a look at the expense that you are contemplating, classify it as an operating or capital expense and prepare your records as follows:

Figure 4.1	Classification of Expenses

Expense: _____ Total $_____ HST/GST $_____ PST$_____

Authorized by: _____ Date Paid: _____

1. What is the classification of the expense?   ☐ Operating   ☐ Capital

2. Will the expense impact future revenues?   _____

3. Is the expense reasonable under the circumstances? Why? _____

4. Will the expense reduce costs to improve bottom lines? _____

5. Is there a personal use component? If so what %? _____

Bookkeeping Standard

We previously asked you to take a look at the Statement of Business Activities and to note that there are a host of expenditures that Revenue Canada considers to be "normal" in the context of most businesses. They have allocated a field code to the expense types. Make sure you claim these if they apply to your business and code all hard copy (the envelope containing all the receipts of one type, for example) with the field code numbers allocated to the expense type. Such a format will make your tax audit a breeze, as every line addressed on the statement will be cross referenced to an envelope, folder, box, etc. that contains the same number.

Personal-Use Standard

Make a list of all expenditures that have both a personal and business component to determine if any of those items are tax deductible, as shown below.

Tax Deductibility Finder   Chart common expenses of the family below, and determine whether any of them should be claimed as a business expense, bearing in mind that they must have a direct bearing on the income-earning activities of the business and reasonable under the circumstances.

| Figure 4.2 | Business Component of Mixed-Use Expenses | | | | |

Expense	Do You Have Receipts?		Can You Claim the Expense?	Can You Use It?	
	Yes	No		Yes	No
A. Personal **Groceries**			Usually no, but entertaining for business purposes is tax deductible (50% usually), so is the expense of feeding children in a babysitting business (100%). Personal use must always be isolated, however.		
Clothing			Usually no, however certain clothing is deductible, provided it is unsuitable for street wear; example, judges' robes; entertainers' costumes. These must be depreciated, rather than written off in full.		
Footware			Usually no, however, employed dancers and certain self-employed taxpayers may make a claim in certain cases if their special footware is "used up" in the pursuit of business income. For example, those who run a winter resort might write off the cost of snowshoes worn by instructors, or ballerinas may write off the cost of their shoes.		
Entertainment			Yes, but generally restricted to 50% of costs; except for events that are staff gatherings — but no more than 6 times a year. If you entertain in your home, keep receipts of food, liquor, etc., specific to the event. Keep entertainment log to record name and address of person being entertained.		
Utilities			Yes, a portion of these expenses are deductible if workspace in home claim is otherwise allowed. Keep total bills, but prorate expenses according to square footage of office space.		
Repairs/ **Maintenance**			Yes, certain employed musicians, other employees, and the self–employed may make this claim for repairs to home office, revenue properties, certain equipment. Personal use must be isolated.		
Mortgage **Payments**			Yes. But only interest costs (not principal) are deductible by the self-employed, according to the space used for business purposes.		
Insurance **Payments**			Yes, if home office claims, musician's instrument costs, auto expense claims and insurance for other equipment costs are otherwise allowable.		
Car Payments			Never for personal driving; however, costs of running an auto are deductible, if used for business or employment purposes and written off according to information on distance travelled in auto log.		

Figure 4.2	Business Component of Mixed-Use Expenses (Cont'd)

Expense	Do You Have Receipts?		Can You Claim the Expense?	Can You Use It?	
	Yes	No		Yes	No
Tuition Fees			Claim as a tax credit rather than a deduction if over $100 and paid to a designated educational institute. Sometimes can be claimed as an expense of business as a training cost, in which case either the credit or the deduction must be chosen. For higher-income earners, the deduction may result in a higher claim.		
Gifts			Personal, no. If made to a client of a self-employed taxpayer, or in some cases, an employed commissioned salesperson, yes. Note gift certificates to restaurants are subject to the 50% restriction on meals.		
Medical/Pharmacy			Claim as a medical expense credit on the return. Group health plan premiums may be a tax deductible business expense starting in 1998.		
B. Employment					
Clothing			No. Not even dry cleaning, cost of special shoes or workboots is allowable.		
Car Expenses			Yes, if Form T2200 is signed and auto log kept up.		
Parking			Yes, if duties include working away from the employer's office to sign contracts on behalf of employer and Form T2200 is available.		
Lunches			Only if away on business for employer for at least 12 hours. Entertainment expenses may be allowed if you are a commission salesperson, for the purposes of entertaining your client .		
Office Supplies			Yes, if used up directly in your job and Form T2200 is signed by the employer.		
Long-Distance Calls			Yes, if made for business or employment purposes. However, monthly rental charges are not deductible unless a separate business line is installed.		
Special Clothing			Generally no, unless unsuitable for street wear, as explained above.		
Tools & Equipment			The self-employed may write off the cost of tools and equipment according to special rules; the employed taxpayer may not, with the exception of claims for auto, musical instruments or aircraft.		
Licences & Bonding			Yes, these costs are deductible by both employed and self-employed persons.		
Computers/Phones			Only the self-employed may write off the costs of these capital assets, including cost of acquisition (usually a capital expense) and interest costs.		

| Figure 4.2 | Business Component of Mixed-Use Expenses (Cont'd) | | | |

Expense	Do You Have Receipts?		Can You Claim the Expense?	Can You Use It?	
	Yes	No		Yes	No
Interest Costs			The self-employed may claim the costs of interest paid on loans to finance their operating costs, equipment purchases and home workspace. Employees may only write off interest costs on auto, aircraft and musical instrument acquisitions, but not mortgage interest or other costs.		
Salary to Assistant			Yes, these costs are deductible by both the employed and self-employed. File form T2200 for the employee.		
Office Rent/ In-Home			These costs are deductible by employed and self-employed. However, for employed taxpayers, there is never an allowable claim for mortgage interest and CCA. Unless you earn commissions you also may not claim property taxes or insurance costs.		
Training Costs			These may be deductible against business income or claimed as a tuition tax credit, if eligible.		
Accounting/Legal Fees			Yes, these are deductible by all taxpayers. However, in the case of employees, the fees must be paid to appeal an assessment of tax; or in cases where you were forced to establish rights to salary, wages or commissions owed to you.		
Income Tax Prep.			Not deductible by employees; however employed commissioned salespeople and the self-employed may make a claim; certain investors also.		
C. Investments Interest Costs			Yes, deductible if there is a potential for the earning of rents, interest or dividends. However, this is true only of loans used to acquire non-registered investments.		
Safety Deposit Box			Yes.		
Management Fees			Yes, but not for registered investments.		
Accounting Fees			Only if accounting is a usual part of the operations of your property.		
Investment Counsel			Yes. For details, obtain Revenue Canada's IT 238.		
D. Self-Employment Operating Expenses			Yes, those expenses "used up" in the running of a business are 100% deductible if reasonable and incurred to earn income from a business with a reasonable expectation of profit.		
Capital Expenses			No. Only a percentage of costs, known as capital cost allowance, may be deducted, at the taxpayer's option, to write down a notional amount for wear and tear of the asset.		

RECAP: 10 Simple Steps To Writing Off More Deductions Without Dramatically Changing Your Life

1. **Establish intent**. When you go into business for yourself, be a pro, if you want to reap serious tax deductions. Establish: do you have a hobby or do you have a business? The test is whether there is a reasonable expectation of profit from the activities. If there is no profit motive, generally no income is reported, no expenses are deductible.

2. **Know the definition: Reasonable Expectation of Profit**. As soon as your "pastime" or hobby results in profit (revenues received exceed expenses), you have a business on your hands and the income from this should be reported. (Otherwise you could face the potential of being charged with gross negligence or tax evasion.) General factors considered by Revenue Canada in assessing reasonable expectation of profit are outlined in IT 504R2:
   - Time devoted to the business
   - Distribution activities: presentation of works, products, services, to the public
   - Time spent in marketing the goods or services of the enterprise
   - Revenues received
   - Historical record of profits
   - Cyclical trends in the business
   - Type of expenses claimed and their relevance to the business
   - Business owner's qualifications to run the business successfully
   - Business owner's membership in professional associations
   - Growth of revenues, taking into account economic conditions, and other market changes.

   Revenue Canada states that none of these has any more weight than the other in determining whether a business has a reasonable expectation of profit. Rather all criteria are analyzed together. Make sure your Daily Business Journal addresses these 10 factors. (Refer back to Chapter 3.)

3. **Establish income sources.** Identify your unique income-earning process, how income will come in, in what amounts and when, by preparing detailed future projections.

4. **Know your profit margins well**. Be prepared to justify there is a reasonable expectation of profit even after you have accounted for the cost of goods sold.

5. **Understand Revenue Canada's written restrictions**. Don't try to claim more than two conventions per year; or 100% of meals and entertainment costs, or 100% of legal fees paid to acquire your office

building. Make it a point to read the published Interpretation Bulletin, Information Circulars and Tax Guides from Revenue Canada which can give you important information about claims for your business. Buy a highlighter pen for sections you wish to discuss with your advisors.

6. **Attach a Tax Saver Stamp** to all invoices and receipts to justify reasonable expectation of profit, personal use components or cost-cutting measures. This is a great way to take a pro-active stance to audit-proofing. Then, **establish a** *Bookkeeping Standard* in your office that's very simple to use and that all staff are required to follow:

   - Get receipts/invoices for all expenditures
   - Classify receipts/invoices
   - Enter into bookkeeping system
   - File in folders/envelopes for tax purposes.

7. **Find the "low-lying fruit".** Are there expenditures you have made that have a business component? If so, are you claiming the business portion of those expenses on your return? Try to turn every expenditure into a legitimate tax deduction. Before you part with future tax dollars, ask yourself, "Is it Deductible?" and if not, why not? Arrange your personal affairs around your business activities to legitimize deductibility of many of your costs. (See Chapter 9.)

8. **Establish your rights to legitimate business losses, and fight for them.** There is no legislated time limit for a "reasonable expectation of profit." If a tax auditor is looking at a period of two to three years only, it is quite possible it is unreasonable of him/her to expect a profit yet. This is very true of business activities undertaken by songwriters, visual and recording artists, writers, farmers, and others. Some of these taxpayers may take years to reach the critical acclaim to be profitable (and for sure, Revenue Canada will be there then to take their share of the profits). Therefore it is most important for you to be able to establish legitimate operating losses that can be carried forward to offset future income. Revenue Canada will not take this right away from you if you can show by addressing the factors described on page 62 that you have conducted your affairs in legitimate efforts to show profits.

9. **Use the Onus of Proof to your advantage.** Before spending another dollar — ever — stop to consider "Is this deductible?" Is there a business purpose attached to the expense? If not, can there be? Make it your goal to arrange your personal affairs around your business acitivities. Remember, the auditor's interpretation comes from an

unfair advantage: hindsight. The onus of proof can actually put the taxpayer in a position of power for two reasons:

- You have the power of vision on your side: you can outline the potential for profit
- You have the position of fairness on your side: ultimately it is unfair for Revenue Canada to judge business decisions in hindsight. There aren't too many taxpayers who actually risk their resources to intentionally lose money.

For these reasons, therefore, you should pursue your rights under the law to claim every one of the business expenses you are entitled to, even those with mixed components of personal and business use. (Also see comments in Chapter 11.)

10. **Arm yourself with the facts**. Find out everything you can about the way Revenue Canada has taxed those in similar ventures. Ask your advisors for information about recent court cases that deal with the issues you face in growing your business. Also, consult your local tax office, obtain a listing of forms and guides, and order the tax-filing forms and guides specific to your venture, together with any Interpretation Bulletins that may affect how you arrange your affairs on an on-going basis to meet the questions of the auditor.

CHAPTER 5

Simple Rules for Writing Off Asset Purchases

"Talent alone won't make you a success. Neither will being in the right place at the right time, unless you are ready. The most import question is: "Are you ready?"
JOHNNY CARSON

KEY CONCEPTS

- Assets used to earn income in a business will often lose their value due to wear and tear
- Revenue Canada allows a "permissive deduction" to account for this loss in value
- Capital Cost Allowance (CCA) is a declining balance method of accounting for depreciation
- Expenses must be capitalized when they have a useful life of more than one year
- Repairs and restoration of an asset to its original condition are 100% deductible.

REAL LIFE: Jared enjoyed his work as a waiter while he attended university. During his days at The Happy Hunter Inn, he encountered many guests, one of whom was a local businessman, Allan Blair; another was a local business woman, Juanita Carez. The usual chit chat between server and client led to a number of interesting conversations. Jared was a computer whiz who specialized in devising policies and procedures for businesses struggling with the ever-changing world of information and communications technology. Before he knew it, he was subcontracting for Allan's company and Juanita's, and reaping the rewards of a job well done. . .further referrals.

Jared found himself, at year end, clearly in business, and with a major tax problem. . .where to start in gathering information about his income and expenses? After meeting with his accountant, he was surprised to find his income records and deductions for operating expenses were in fairly good order. What he needed to look for to complete his tax return, was the details about the assets he had acquired in his business: his computer, his office furniture, his desk, his car and his professional library.

THE PROBLEM

Jared's accountant was trying to save him tax dollars by scheduling his assets used in the business. Problem was. . .he bought some new, some used; and his parents gave him the rest of it. How to schedule these business assets involved not just receipting, but also looking for Fair Market Valuations. How was he supposed to get that? Also, for what? He wasn't even sure he knew what this CCA was all about!

THE SOLUTION

Jared's accountant did another wise thing: he sat Jared down and gave him a crash course in Capital Cost Allowance. . .the deduction allowed to acknowledge the wear and tear on business assets used to produce income. By knowing how assets are written off for tax purposes, he knew he would help Jared make wise tax-oriented decisions about spending his money in the future.

THE PARAMETERS

An income-producing asset used in a business can be "written down" to acknowledge depreciation due to its use. No one really knows for sure what the value of an asset is at any given point in time. This will only be realized upon disposition — when the owner sells the asset, or disposes of it in another way — like converting it to personal use or transferring it to a relative, for example.

Therefore, the acknowledgement of the cost of depreciation of assets, for tax purposes is really an educated guess. Revenue Canada has done some of that guesswork for you by prescribing special classes and rates for the assets to fall into, in creating a systematic procedure called "Capital Cost Allowance." CCA is a deduction from business income, subject to special rules. The CCA deduction can often be inadequately or incorrectly used by taxpayers, with the result that tax is overpaid in the long run. Some parameters for avoiding this are outlined below:

Accuracy of Claims Is Important

CCA is known as a "permissive deduction." The claim is made at the taxpayer's option, however, there is a special rule the taxpayer must know about to manage the account properly. This is significant because the taxpayer must be sure to make the claim properly, or if a mistake was made, notify Revenue Canada immediately. That's because the adjustment period for permissive deductions like CCA is only 90 days after receipt of the Notice of Assessment or Reassessment, rather than the normal adjustment period, which goes all the way back to 1985 for most other federal tax provisions. (Although tax auditors have been known to allow retractive CCA claims when a file is audited.)

Capitalize Expenditures With Life Spans of More Than One Year

Generally, assets with a useful and enduring life such as automobiles, trucks, machinery and buildings are considered capital expenditures, that must be scheduled for CCA purposes. Their costs may not be written off in full in the same way that other operating expenses are. This is where many taxpayers make expensive mistakes. Jared, for example, thought he could write off the full $3,000 he spent on his computer system. Unfortunately only a fraction of the expenditure would be allowed this year.

Capitalize Expenditures With Values Over $200

Even though small equipment and supplies may have a useful life of more than one year, if their value is under $200 they can generally be written off as operating expenses. Examples of such items are calculators, pencil sharpeners and desk lamps.

Know When Repairs Are Capitalized

Does the repair of an asset add to its useful life? If so, the amounts are likely added to the capital cost of the asset. Does the repair, on the other hand, simply put the asset back to its original condition? In that case, we generally write off the costs in full. For example, replacing the shingles that blew off the business premises during a windstorm would be fully deductible, whereas replacing the whole roof would be treated as a capital expenditure.

Know Your Basic CCA Rate Structure

CCA is also known as the diminishing-balance method of claiming depreciation. This means that a fixed maximum percentage is applied against the balance of the capital cost of the asset remaining at the end of each year. To arrive at this fixed percentage, assets of a similar type are classified or "pooled" into specific classes for CCA purposes. Your tax advisor will have a complete listing, as will Revenue Canada's business guides.

Know About the "Half-Year Rules"

When assets are acquired, the "Cost of Additions," which generally includes both GST/HST and PST, is recorded on the CCA schedule. A "half-year rule" is then applied to most assets. That is, in the year of acquisition, the CCA rate can be applied only to half the cost of the asset.

Certain Assets Are Exempt From the Half-Year Rules

Class 12 assets, other than computer software, a television commercial message, certain assets acquired from related persons and a video cassette acquired after February 15, 1984, for rental to persons for less than seven days a month are all examples of assets not subject to the half-year rule.

Cost of Additions

The "cost of additions" includes taxes and freight charges. Things are a bit more complicated when the properties are acquired through a "deemed disposition," such as on the death of a taxpayer, or a "change in use" from personal to business use. In that case, deemed dispositions or transfers are valued at **Fair Market Value (FMV);** that is, what a willing buyer would pay a willing seller for the asset on the open market. There are special rules when the amount received for the asset is inadequate, especially between related parties, when trade-in values are below FMV or if assets are disposed of at a superficial loss. See *Jacks on Tax Savings* and *The Complete Canadian Home Business Guide to Taxes*, both by Evelyn Jacks, for more details.

Short Fiscal Years

Here is an important rule for start-up businesses: the CCA claim is generally prorated when there is a short fiscal year. This means that if you started your business on July 1, and had a December 31 fiscal year end, only 50% of the normal available depreciation deduction allowed can be claimed. If you started your business on September 1, only one third of the normal CCA deduction is claimable, and so on.

Cost of Borrowing to Buy Assets

Interest costs to buy assets used in a business will be tax deductible as an operating expense of the business. If there is a personal component to the use of the asset, the interest, like other related expenses, must be prorated. Many taxpayers don't know about this little rule: the taxpayer can choose to capitalize any annual financing fees paid for the assets, simply by adding the cost on to the undepreciated capital cost of the asset, in order to preserve more of those costs for future use, when profits are perhaps higher. To do so, the taxpayer must make an election under Subsection 21(3).

Handling Dispositions

It is advisable to consult your tax advisor in order to calculate the most advantageous procedure to follow when disposing of assets, depending on the circumstances, as income inclusions or certain deductions can result when all assets of a class are disposed of.

Remember that dispositions could occur due to sale, but also due to other circumstances, such transfer of assets to another or to personal use, or cessation of business due to death, or emigration. In those latter instances, called "deemed dispositions," FMV of the asset must be determined.

Computer Upgrading Challenges Are Recognized

There are two special rules that allow for a fast write-off of computer equipment. One deals with the problem of obsolescence; the other with Year 2000 compliance.

Obsolescence   Computers and their related systems software are usually placed in Class 10 and depreciated at a rate of 30%. Other office equipment often falls into Class 8. Like equipment is "pooled" within its respective class and CCA is taken at your option, based on the Undepreciated Capital Cost (UCC) of all the assets in the particular class. A full tax write-off (terminal loss) can only be taken once all the assets of the class are disposed of at an amount less than UCC. For more details, consult your tax advisor.

Year 2000 Compliance   The Department of Finance has devised a 100% deduction for businesses that replace existing non-compliant equipment with Year 2000 compliant equipment through the Capital Cost Allowance structure. That means the deduction is still at your option for equipment acquired in the period January 1, 1998, to June 30, 1999. Ask your tax advisor about this.

Computer Software

If you acquire a program that has a lasting and enduring benefit, it will be classified in Class 12 — 100% depreciation rate. This software would, however, be subject to the "half-year rule." If there is no lasting and enduring benefit — for example, the software is considered to be an operational expense — a full tax deduction is possible. Systems software is generally classed in Class 10 and depreciated at a rate of 30%. Remember, if it costs more than $1,000, it will qualify for inclusion in a separate Class 10.

Patents and Licences

Innovators have some interesting rules to contend with in writing off their patents and licences. These are usually written off on a straight-line basis over the life of the patent or licence. That is, if you paid $15,000 for a patent for a period of 15 years, the depreciation would be $1,000 a year. Licences of an indefinite period are classed as "eligible capital property." Three-quarters of the costs may be written off on a 7% declining balance. For all patents and rights to use patented information acquired after April 26, 1993, a CCA class is available with a 25% declining-balance rate.

Separate Classes for Certain Auto

Automobiles are generally classified in Class 10, at a CCA rate of 30%. These are usually known as "motor vehicles," and all like assets are pooled together in this class. An exception to the "pooling" rule applies to autos classified to be luxury or "passenger vehicles." Each such vehicle used for business purposes is placed into its own Class 10.1, which also features a CCA rate of 30%. However, there are deductibility restrictions on CCA, interest and lease costs. For example, since January 1, 1998, the maximum capital cost has been $26,000 plus taxes. This means that if you buy a $50,000 car, you can only take a CCA deduction based on a value of $26,000 plus taxes, if it is a passenger vehicle. The half-year rule also applies on acquisition of the vehicle, in the year of disposition. More on this in Chapter 6.

Separate Classes for Certain Buildings

Pooling is not allowed in cases where a taxpayer owns a number of rental properties, each with a capital cost of $50,000 or more. In such cases, each building is listed in a separate class (usually Class 1 — 4%). Where the taxpayer owns a condominium or row-housing structure, the aggregate cost of all the units in a building will become one class for each group of structures that costs $50,000 or more.

GST/HST Exceptions.

The Input Tax Credits (ITCs) received by a business registered to collect the GST/HST will have an impact on the "Cost of Additions." For example, assets classified as "Capital Personal Properties" for GST/HST purposes (those used 51% or more for business use) qualify for a full input tax credit of GST/HST paid. Once received, such an input tax credit must *reduce* the capital cost of the asset used for capital cost allowance purposes. Therefore, it is important to keep track of ITCs received specifically for capital assets. For more details see *Jacks on Tax Savings* by Evelyn Jacks.

TAX ADVISOR

It is very important for small business owners to plan asset acquisitions and dispositions carefully. The first thing you should set up is a tracking system, as shown on the following page. The CCA schedule, which is used to compute your CCA deduction, is shown below. Notice the important figures: your CCA deduction and the UCC or Undepreciated Capital Cost. This UCC figure is what you'll base next year's CCA deduction on. It will be increased by any future additions, and decreased by future dispositions:

Figure 5.1   CCA Schedule

Class	UCC	Additions	Dispositions	New UCC (A)	Half Year Adj.	CCA Base Amt.	Rate	CCA (B)	UCC (A–B)

Total CCA: $ _____

Figure 5.2   Asset Tracking System for Tax Purposes

ASSETS PURCHASED/SOLD
TAX YEAR _____

A. ADDITIONS OF ASSETS: EQUIPMENT BOUGHT

Date	Asset Type	Description	Total Cost	Personal Portion	GST/HST	PST

B. DISPOSITIONS OF ASSETS

Date	Asset	Description	Original Cost	Proceeds	GST/HST	PST

C. LAND ACQUISITION/DISPOSITION DETAILS: Note land is not a depreciable asset.

Date	Description	Total Cost	Proceeds of Disposal	Personal Portion	GST/HST	PST

Planning Opportunities Using the CCA Claim

Next, ask your tax advisor about the following:

- in year of acquisition
- in year of disposition
- when an asset appreciates in value
- when an asset depreciates more than the prescribed rate
- business is very low
- when net income is anticipated to be much higher next year
- when it is your goal to increase RRSP contributions.

Buy vs. Lease

There is always the question of the benefits of buying an asset vs. the benefits of leasing it. There are two points to consider:

- **Your marginal tax rate.** Not only do you need to know that your income will support the leasing payments or interest costs, but you'll need to know the true dollar value of the deduction. Here's an example, using the acquisition of a motor vehicle, when the marginal tax rate is 26%; assuming 100% business use.

Figure 5.3	Tax Cost Analysis: Motor Vehicles			
How?	**Tax Provision**	**Write-off in Yr. 1**	**Write-off in Yr. 2**	**Dollar Value of Tax Write-off @ 26%**
Buy	CCA on auto total cost of $25,000	$3,750	$6,375	Yr. 1 = $ 975; Yr. 2 = $1,658
	Interest on car loan @ 6%	$1,500	$1,350	Yr. 1 = $ 390; Yr. 2 = $ 351
Lease	Monthly leasing costs	$6,000	$6,000	Each year $1,560

So, if this taxpayer bought the car and took out a car loan to do so, his tax write-offs in Year 1 would amount to $3,750 + $1,500 = $5,250 and the real dollar value of those write-offs would be $975 + $390 for a total of $1,365. Leasing the vehicle would bring a real dollar saving of $1,560; so the taxpayer in this case gets a bigger benefit by leasing, in the amount of $195 in Year 1.

In Year 2, there is no "half-year rule" on the bought asset. Therefore the real dollar value of the tax write-offs for CCA and interest is a total of $2,009; of the leased option, it's $1,560, so the CCA/interest claim is better.

One must also take into account, however, the cost and cash flow available under each option, assuming the identical vehicle is purchased.

Have your tax advisor prepare a chart that looks like this, to help you make the decision:

Figure 5.3	Before-Tax Earnings Chart		
		Year 1	**Year 2**
Cash to be generated to pay for the car bought with a car loan:			
Interest amounts		$_____	$_____
Principal Amounts		$_____	$_____
Total		$_____	$_____
Cash to be generated to pay for the leased car		$_____	$_____
Before-tax earnings required		$_____	$_____

Which option can you best afford?

Your Balance Sheet   Take into account the effect of asset acquisition methods on your balance sheet, and the overall fiscal health of your business. Will a lender, for example, finance your leasing costs with an operating line? Or is it easier for the lender to provide you with a loan for a specific asset purchase? This will have a bearing on your decision making as well as the tax implications.

RECAP: A Dozen Tips For Writing Off Your Asset Purchases

1. **Always file your tax return on time.** Changes to permissive deductions like CCA have a time limit: adjustments can only be made within 90 days of receipt of the Notice of Assessment or Reassessment.

2. **Never claim capital assets as operating expenses.** 100% write-offs are not allowed on the purchase or improvement of assets with a useful life of more than one year. This is an expensive mistake that can cost you interest dollars.

3. **Schedule the cost of improvements to assets.** Restoration of the asset to its original condition is deductible. The cost of improving the asset is generally capitalized.

4. **Classify your assets correctly**. Make sure you know the CCA rate that will be applied to the new asset you are thinking of purchasing, and whether there is an exemption for the half-year rule.

5. **Prorate your CCA claim in the first year of business**. CCA rates and the half-year rule apply to businesses who are in existence for a full fiscal year. This means that a business that started mid-way through

a fiscal year, must prorate the calculated CCA claim by the number of days the business was operating.

6. **Consider capitalizing the interest costs if business is losing money.** This is a great way to preserve the costs for use in the future when income may be higher.

7. **Consider the effects of disposing of all the assets of a class.** Recapture will increase your net profits; terminal losses will decrease them. Do some tax planning to assess proper tax timing of dispositions, if this makes sense otherwise (i.e., the buyer is co-operative).

8. **Be aware of special tax provisions for asset purchases.** The government often provides tax incentives for those who invest in new assets in their business. Recently, a special claim was announced for those businesses replacing hardware in anticipation of Year 2000 compliance problems. Check out the latest interpretations of recent federal and provincial budget provisions with your tax advisor before purchasing new assets.

9. **Track GST/HST paid carefully.** If you are a GST/HST registrant, you'll be able to claim back the cost of your taxes paid on the asset against your GST/HST remittances. This can give your cash flow an important boost, so don't forget to give this information to your tax advisor. Complete the CCA tracking system suggested on page 71 to make sure all the information you need to properly file your income tax return as well as your GST/HST return is available.

10. **Always prorate your maximum CCA deduction for any personal use of the asset.**

11. **Always prepare a tax and cash-flow comparison** of the costs before you make the decision to buy or lease an asset.

12. **Bring details of your asset acquisitions and dispositions** to your tax advisor each and every year. This includes what happened during the tax year, as well as previous asset tracking worksheets.

CHAPTER 6

Maximize Home Office and Auto Expense Benefits

"The person who makes no mistakes, does not usually make anything."
WILLIAM CONNOR MAGEE

KEY CONCEPTS

- Auto expenses are calculated after other operating expenses to adjust for the personal use component of the use of the asset
- Home workspace expenses are calculated last, as they may not be used at all, if they increase or create an operating loss
- Auto logs to record both business and personal use of the vehicle are mandatory to pass a tax auditor's scrutiny
- Deductible auto expenses break down into two groups: operating expenses and fixed costs, the latter of which are usually subject to a maximum deduction
- Home workplace expenses are based on the square footage of an exclusively set-aside space used as the principal business location or on a regular and continuous basis to see customers.

REAL LIFE: Tom, a high school teacher, taught art and woodworking during the day, and built beautiful furniture in his spare time. Over the years, as he perfected his craft, people would marvel at the beautiful pieces in his home and beg him to consider designing and crafting something special for them too. Tom's hobby quickly flourished into a business with a potential for profit. In fact, he had visions of opening a furniture store one day, specializing in Santa Fe pieces.

THE PROBLEM

At tax-filing time Tom wondered about the $3,500 he had received for making a piece of furniture for his neighbours, the Smiths. Should he report the income? If so, are there expenses he can claim to offset his income? For example, can he claim the costs of setting up his workshop, his tools and the varnish he uses to finish the furniture? What about the trips back and forth to pick up supplies. Are they deductible?

THE SOLUTION

As you know from prior chapters, tax deductions are created by virtue of the fact that there is a potential for income. In fact, Revenue Canada's IT334 explains:

> "In order for any activity or pursuit to be regarded as a source of income, there must be a reasonable expectation of profit.
>
> Where such an expectation does not exist (as is the case with most hobbies), neither amounts received nor expenses incurred are included in the income computation for tax purposes and any excess of expenses over receipts is a personal or living expense, the deduction of which is denied. . .
>
> On the other hand, if the hobby or pastime results in receipts of revenue in excess of expenses, that fact is a strong indication that the hobby is a venture with an expectation of profit.

These interpretations leave taxpayers like Tom with no choice but to compute whether there is indeed an excess of income over expenses. To start this process, receipts must be gathered for operating expenses, like the varnish, paint, paint remover, brushes, etc. in Tom's case.

Tom must also know how to compute two other important deductions: his auto expenses and his home office expenses.

THE PARAMETERS

The specific deductions that any business may take should be made in the following order:

- Costs of goods sold
- Operating expenses
- Auto expenses
- Capital Cost Allowance
- Home office expenses.

Cost of goods sold reduces gross profits on the Statement of Business Activities to account for purchases of goods that will be resold. This computation appears first on the statement to properly account for margin levels in the assessment of reasonable expectation of profits.

Other operating expenses come next. This is for things that are "used up" in the business: advertising, supplies, rents, salaries, and so on. These amounts are 100% deductible if there is a reasonable expectation of profit from the venture, and can be used to offset other income of the year if the operating expenses exceed revenues for the year.

Auto expenses are claimed next, because they contain a capital cost allowance component, if the taxpayer owns the car. Start by claiming operating expenses of the car, together with interest costs (see worksheet on page 82). The owner can then decide, based on whether or not an operating loss already exists, whether to claim the deduction for CCA.

Next, one takes a close look at other assets. Should the deduction for CCA be taken for these assets? It is possible that the owner may wish to create a larger tax loss, if other income sources of the year, like pension or interest income, for example, are high, or if the owner wants to carry excess losses back to any one of the prior three taxation years. This is a way to recover previously paid taxes. Or the owner may wish to save the CCA deduction for a future date, when income is higher.

Finally, one comes to the deduction of the home workspace expenses. There is an important rule to remember in claiming these amounts, which warrant their ordering position at the end of the process: you may not increase or create an operating loss by taking a deduction for home workspace expenses.

TAX ADVISOR

There are special requirements to be met when claiming common business expenses like the costs of running your car and the costs of keeping a workspace in the home. It is most important that they are observed, as the deductions are both lucrative and frequently audited.

Automobile Expenses

Almost every small business owner claims auto expenses against the revenues of the business. However, this line is also the subject of more failures than any other on a tax audit. The main tax-filing traps are ones taxpayers must assume responsibility for. They fail to keep receipts and keep a record of their travels.

Now, this "auto log" cannot just record business driving. You must also show the auditor how many kilometres were driven in the entire year. Many, no most, taxpayers have trouble keeping this log. Yet it's mandatory and will cause your claims to be reduced or disallowed completely if you don't have one.

For this reason, it's a good idea to keep your business kilometres driven in your Daily Business Journal. Before you leave your home office (see below), make sure your record the kilometres when you start. Then make a point of charting your business driving during the day, which for most small business owners means that the full day of driving is technically deductible.

What's not allowed is the distances you drive to pick up milk on the way home. That's personal driving, unless of course, the post-office where you pick up your business mail is in the grocery store in which you buy the milk.

So it's important to isolate the personal portions of any of your driving in order to give the auditor an accurate picture of the business use of your auto.

Also allowed is a reasonable estimation of coin car washes and coin telephone calls. However, when people log these actual amounts, usually they find they are underestimating their expenses.

Figure 6.1 Auto Log Summary

Month	Km Bus	Km Pers	Km Total	Gas	M & R	Park	Wash	Ins.	Int.	Other: (Explain)	$
Jan											
Feb											
Mar											
Apr											
May											
Jun											
Jul											
Aug											
Sep											
Oct											
Nov											
Dec											
Total											

REAL LIFE: Assume Guam, who is a self-employed hairdresser, drove 15,000 km this year for business purposes, out of 20,000 km driven in total. His total expenses for the car were $7,500. Using the following formula, Guam would compute the tax-deductible portion of his expenses:

$$\frac{\text{Total Business Kilometres}}{\text{Total Kilometres Driven in Year}} \times \text{Total Expenses} = \text{Deductible Expenses}$$

$$\frac{15,000}{20,000} \times \$7,500 = \$5,625$$

The deductible amount is therefore $5,625.

The actual expenditures that you have for your car during the year are classified into two groups:

Operating Expences
- Gas and Oil
- Maintenance and Repairs
- Tire purchases
- Insurance and Licence Fees
- Auto club premiums
- Car washes

Fixed Expenses
- Interest costs
- Leasing costs
- Capital cost allowances

The operating expenses are straightforward: keep the receipts, total them and claim a portion of them according to the business-use fraction determined by your travel log.

The fixed expenses will be subject to the proration as well; however, they are separated because there have been certain claim limitations attached to them over the past several years:

As you can see, there was a significant development in tax law on June 17, 1987, the day of the last major Tax Reform. That was the day the Finance Minister announced the concept of "Passenger Vehicles." A passenger vehicle, in tax jargon is also considered to be a "luxury vehicle."

Figure 6.2	Maximum Deductible Costs of Passenger Vehicle		
Date	**Interest Costs**	**Leasing Costs**	**CCA**
After June 17, 1987 and before Sept. 1, 1989	$8.33 a day	$600 a month	$20,000
After Aug. 31, 1989 and before 1997	$10.00 a day	$650 a month plus taxes	$24,000 plus taxes
Jan. 1 to Dec. 31, 1997	$8.33 a day	$550 a month plus taxes	$25,000 plus taxes
Jan. 1, 1998 to Dec. 31, 1999	$8.33 a day	$650 a month plus taxes	$26,000 plus taxes

That is, the government decided that tax write-offs for the fixed costs for passenger vehicles would be limited to certain ceiling levels, as outlined above.

So, if for example, you buy a new car for a total of $30,000 plus taxes, the maximum claim you can make for capital cost allowance purposes in 1998 was a total of $26,000 plus federal and provincial sales taxes.

If you leased a vehicle for, say $750, the most you could write off for tax purposes was $650 a month plus federal and provincial taxes.

And if you paid the bank an interest charge on the loan you took to buy your car, your maximum interest expense deduction is limited to $8.33 a day or about $250 a month. Take these restrictions into account before making your buying decisions.

In fact, you might ask yourself whether paying $40,000 for a car is really worth it, if *it's not deductible!*

*To take that thought one step further. . .*does it make sense to buy a new car at all? If, for example, a new car costs $40,000, but the same model two years old costs $25,000, what's the better decision? From a tax viewpoint, it's the $25,000 car (but ask them to throw in a bumper-to-bumper three year warranty!).

If your car is not classified a "passenger vehicle," it will be called a "motor vehicle" for tax purposes. That means the car is not subject to the passenger vehicle restrictions. Such a vehicle can either be one that is below the cost factors outlined above. Or it may exceed the cost limits but have an allowable "use factor." For example, you can avoid the restrictions with:

- A pick-up truck that seats one to three people used more than 50% of the time to transport goods or equipment
- A pick-up truck, sport utility or other van that seats four to nine people used 90% of the time or more to transport goods, equipment or passengers
- A farm truck used primarily (more than 50% of the time) to transport goods or equipment, or more than 90% of the time to transfer goods, equipment or people for the purposes of earning income.

Claiming Capital Cost Allowances (CCA)   The CCA classification used for a Motor Vehicle is Class 10, with a depreciation rate of 30%. You may have many different vehicles in this class, providing they each fall under the restricted values defined above. Acquisitions increase the value of the CCA pool, dispositions decrease the pool, and only when all the assets of the class are disposed of are there recapture or terminal loss consequences. See Chapter 7 for explanations of these terms.

A Passenger Vehicle is classified in Class 10.1, which also has a depreciation rate of 30%. However, all Class 10.1 assets must be listed separately, rather than pooled together in one class. In the year of acquisition, the normal "half-year rules" apply to both Class 10 and Class 10.1. That is, only 50% of the normal capital cost allowance is claimed in the year of acquisition.

As mentioned earlier, your CCA deduction is always claimed at your option, so if your other business expenses are already high enough to reduce income to the desired level, you can choose to "save" the higher Undepreciated Capital Cost to another year.

Dispositions   Here are two more points to remember regarding passenger vehicles:

- there is a "half-year rule on sale" of a passenger vehicle. That is, you will be able to claim 50% of the capital cost allowance that would be normally allowed if you owned the vehicle at the end of the year.
- terminal loss is not deductible and recapture is not reportable on Class 10.1 vehicles. This means you should keep a close eye on the value of your luxury vehicle, and consider whether it makes sense to trade it in, if it drops too far below your allowable depreciated value.

Note that in the case of Class 10 vehicles, there is no half-year rule on disposition, but generally no terminal loss is allowed if you didn't take enough depreciation. Recapture on Class 10 assets will, however, have to be accounted for.

More Than One Vehicle   Things can get somewhat complicated if you use more than one vehicle in the business. For example, let's say you own a florist business, have a delivery van, but also use your personal vehicle to give quotes and make supply runs. In that case, the costs of the van would not normally be subject to prorations or restrictions if it was used full-time for delivery of flowers. The driving with the personal car would obviously have a business component, which could be deductible if you kept the distance records.

In fact if you use your spouse's car occasionally for your business affairs, keep track of the distance driven. Use those distance points to reduce your overall expenses. To be completely accurate, you can keep separate distance logs for each vehicle. This would enable you to claim a portion of annual costs, like insurance, for example, on both vehicles.

Here's what a typical auto worksheet would look like, with information taken from the distance log (see sample summation following) and saved receipts:

Figure 6.3	Worksheet for Deductible Auto Expenses

Distance Log:

Total kilometres driven to earn income	15,896
Total kilometres driven in the year	22,554

Operating Expenses		**Fixed Costs**	
Gas and Oil	$1,527.00	Insurance	$1,250.00
Repairs/Maintenance	2,456.00	License	48.00
Car Washes	150.00	Interest	3,000.00
Motor League Auto Club	65.25	CCA from schedule	3,750.00
Total	$4,198.25	Total	$8,048.00

Total Auto Expenses	Operating Expenses	$ 4,198.25
	Fixed Costs	8,048.00
	Total	$12,246.25

Personal Use Component	(3,615.13)

Deductible Auto Expenses	$ 8,631.12

Home Workspace Expenses

It is relatively easy to make the claim for home workspace expenses. Whether you have a workshop in which you build furniture or a show-room for your Christmas wreathes and candles, keep all of your receipts for all utilities, mortgage interest, property taxes, insurance, maintenance and repairs for the whole home. Then prorate these by the fraction that you obtain with the following information:

$$\frac{\text{Square footage of home workspace}}{\text{Square footage of entire living area}} \times \frac{\text{Total Expenditures}}{\text{Allowed}} = \frac{\text{Deductible}}{\text{Portion}}$$

When computing the entire living area of the home, it is usual to exclude bathrooms and closets. When allocating areas for home with an unfinished or partially finished basement, only include the square footage of the areas that constitute "living area." That would usually include the area in which the wash is done, but not unfinished areas or storage space.

If part of the home was used for storage of business items, like lumber in a carpentry business or boxes of goods for resale, this area would be added both to the home workspace area and to the entire square footage of the home. Where someone uses a garage as a workshop, the square footage of the garage is added to both the numerator and the denominator, and so on.

Total expenditures can include the following:

- Heating costs
- Electricity
- Insurance
- Maintenance
- Mortgage interest
- Property taxes
- Cleaning costs

These items are totalled for the year, and then prorated according to the home workspace ratio. Example:

Figure 6.4	Worksheet for Deductible Home Workspace Expenses

Home workspace ratio:

Home workspace area	250 sq. ft.
Living area of the home	2,400 sq. ft.

Operating Expenses:

Heating costs	$ 1,632
Electricity	1,245
Insurance	895
Maintenance	1,496
Mortgage interest	8,479
Property taxes	4,532
Total	$18,279

Calculation of Allowable Claim:

Total	$18,279	
Less personal portion	16,375	(2,150/2,400 × $18,279)
Allowable Claim	$ 1,904	

There are three more things you need to know to claim home workspace costs properly:

1. You may only claim home workspace expenses if the office is used as follows:

- exclusively to earn business income on a regular and continuous basis for meeting clients, customers or patients; or
- as the principal place of business of the individual.

To clarify, under the first criteria, one or more rooms are set aside solely or exclusively for income-producing purposes. This means, it can't be your living room, or a desk in your bedroom, without a specifically defined, partitioned-off area.

As well, the space must be used to regularly meet customers at some level of frequency, which will be determined according to the type of business and individual facts of each taxpayer upon audit. Therefore, it would be most important to keep a log of appointments to justify these claims.

So for example, a chiropractor who has an office downtown where she sees patients, as well as one at home, would have to justify the home workspace claim by showing that clients regularly attended the home office for treatment. This is best done with a home office appointment log.

Another business, a self-employed editor, for example, would not normally see clients in her home, but would still be entitled to make a claim as it is her primary place of business.

Meeting this second criteria may be more difficult for some. For example, a plumber may make a legitimate claim for home workspace expenses despite the fact that he usually works away from the home workspace. This claim will be allowed if there is no other principal place of business to prepare books, take appointments, prepare quotations, and so on.

2. You do not use the claim to increase or create an operating loss in the business.

Example 1:	Operating profit before home workspace	=	$3,500
	Home workspace expenses		$2,000
	Net profit		$1,500

This claim is OK as a loss is neither created or increased.

Example 2:	Operating profit before home workspace	=	$1,000
	Home workspace expenses		$2,000
	Net profit		($1,000)

This claim is not OK as a loss was created using home workspace expenses. The claim must be adjusted as follows:

Operating profit before home workspace	=	$1,000
Allowable Claim for home workspace		$1,000 only
Adjusted net profit		Nil
Carry-forward of home workspace expenses		$1,000

3. You can and should audit-proof your home workspace claim. Sketch out the office area and its relationship to the living area in the rest of the house. Keep this in your tax files in case of a tax audit, to be used to justify the percentage of tax deductible expenditures that you have claimed. In all cases, expenses claimed as deductions must be reasonable.

RECAP: 8 Easy Steps To Writing Off Auto and Home Office Expenses

1. **Prepare a preliminary Business Statement** for any independent income sources received during the year from the sale of goods made from the home or service provided. If a profit motive is found to exist — i.e., income has the potential to exceed expenses — your hobby could very well be a viable business income source, against which you can claim a series of deductions.

2. **Know how to order your deductions**. Claim cost of goods sold first, then operating expenses, auto expenses, other capital cost allowances and finally home office expenses. That's because CCA is claimed at your option, and home office expenses can be carried forward for use in offsetting business profits next year.

3. **Keep an Auto Log.** It's mandatory during a tax audit.

4. **Keep a log of cash expenditures for your car.** This includes coin car washes, parking meters. Revenue Canada allows a reasonable estimate, but a log will likely produce higher claims.

5. **Know your auto expense restrictions.** Fixed expenses like interest costs, leasing costs and capital cost allowances on your vehicle will be subject to restrictions if you exceed certain value limits. Check these out before making the decision to buy or lease.

6. **Sketch out your home office.** Make sure you can justify your home office claims by drawing a sketch of the office and how it relates in size to the rest of the living area of the home.

7. **Keep an Appointment Log for your home office.** This is particularly important if you also have an office downtown, for example. You must be seen to use the home workspace either as the principal

place of business, or exclusively to earn business income on a regular and continuous basis for meeting clients, customers or patients.

8. **Never increase or create an operating loss from the business with home office claims.** They will be disallowed and you could forget to claim the carry-forward of these expenses to income in future years.

CHAPTER 7

Profiles of the Self-Employed

*"I do the very best I know how — the very best I can; and
I mean to keep on doing so until the end."*
ABRAHAM LINCOLN

KEY CONCEPTS

- Every small business has a unique tax-filing profile with specific circumstances that may warrant special tax treatment
- Like industries generally have like tax-filing profiles when it comes to
  reporting income, deductions and asset acquisitions/dispositions
- Knowing your tax-filing profile can help you explain why certain
  spending patterns are appropriate for your type of enterprise
- Because the "reasonable expectation of profit test" has no set time
  limit, profiling activities can help you argue in favour of the specific
  circumstances your industry grouping faces
- Profiling your business enterprise can help you tax cost average.

REAL LIFE: Marcie runs a babysitting enterprise out of her home. Her husband Jim, is a full-time farmer. Between the two of them, keeping up with
the changing tax rules has been a challenge. They each use their cars in business; to pick up supplies, meet prospective clients and conduct the affairs of
their respective operations.

Marcie is a multi-faceted individual. She helps out where she can: daily
she works in Jim's business as the bookkeeper, where she is paid a salary as
an employee. She is also an accomplished singer/song-writer. One of her
pieces is being reviewed by a major record company and a television net-
work, as her specialty is writing children's songs.

Jim's affairs are such that his start-up years were very lean. He is carrying
forward unused losses of $38,000. This year was a banner year; unfortu-
nately world market activities have reduced pricing to such an extent, Jim is
worried he won't be able to meet his commitments. He is now contemplating a partnership with a neighbour and/or the possibility of selling the farmland, which is extremely valuable, just to make ends meet.

THE PROBLEM

This couple already has an interesting tax situation. However, with change on the horizon, there may be a few more tax twists along the way. Marcie is an employee, but also runs two businesses of her own. In the meantime, Jim needs to maximize his tax write-offs for today and the future, to pull out of his farming enterprise with the greatest success over the long run.

THE SOLUTION

This couple should get some advice from a qualified tax professional who can look at not only the current year results, but the carry-over years — three years back and ten years forward — in assessing future business decisions. In each of their enterprises, special tax rules exist, for both the earning of profits and the appreciation of equity.

THE PARAMETERS

Revenue Canada tells us in the document *Compliance: From Vision to Strategy* that it uses aggregate Statistics Canada data and compares it with information collected internally to identify unreported income. It works with industry associations and like businesses to define a "profile" of the commonalities in income reporting, deductions, and asset acquisitions/dispositions.

Therefore, it's important that you and your advisor identify the taxpayer profile that you and your business fit into, and discuss what basic and industry-specific reporting rules you'll be required to follow, based on special provisions outlined in the Income Tax Act, as well as Revenue Canada's forms and interpretation bulletins.

Next, it is important to flesh out your tax-filing profile with the circumstances specific to the way you run your business. For example, a self-employed editor would spend more on couriers or communications costs, while an in-home footcare specialist would likely claim larger amounts for auto expenses and medical supplies. Both these taxpayers would likely file similar home office claims, though, and be subject to a maximum capital cost allowance ceiling on their automobile values.

Both these taxpayers would also want to overview their current tax-filing obligations in order to properly assess their RRSP contribution limits; and other investment opportunities. Because entrepreneurs must be visionary and forward-looking in planning for their next income sources, it makes sense for them to anticipate changes within their ventures. For this reason, the self-employed taxpayer is in an excellent position to explore and define potential tax results before making any financial moves. To gather the right information to do so, one must possess the knowledge to ask intelligent questions of professional advisors. However, certain information must be gathered and presented, so that the advisor can do a better job.

Following is an overview of taxation parameters for five different tax-filing profiles: the one-person operation or sole proprietorship, the business partnership, the self-employed artist/writer, the self-employed babysitter and the farming proprietorship. You will notice that each has specific tax rules designed to address the nature of the different enterprises. In addition, you'll see certain similarities in the tax-filing framework of the self-employed, as outlined below:

- Methods of Reporting Income
- Deduction of Operating Expenses
- Computation of Capital Cost Allowances
- Computation of Auto Expenses
- Computation of Home Workspace Costs
- Personal Use Allocation.

Sole Proprietorship

Most small businesses start as a "one-person show." From landing the first contract to buying the new computer, or hiring the first employee, these small businesses have true grit. . .and true tax audit problems, if they don't conform to the rules. Income must be reported and deductions calculated on the Business Activities Statement before subtracting home office and personal use to arrive at Net Income. Consider the tips listed in Figure 7.1 as you get started.

- If your gross revenues exceed $30,000 you'll need to register to collect and remit GST/HST in most industries. You may elect to register to obtain a refund of any GST/HST you paid (called input tax credits) on your business inputs. Speak to your tax advisor about the details of this obligation.
- For the sole partnership, Capital Cost Allowances, Auto Expenses and Home Workspace claims are all calculated on separate schedules, as discussed in previous chapters. However, a quick review follows:

Capital Cost Allowances　When you acquire assets with a useful life of more than one year, that generally cost $200 or more, you must schedule

Figure 7.1	The Tax-Filing Framework of the Self-Employed

Transaction	Tax Tip
Income Reporting	Report income on the "accrual" basis. That is, include it in the taxation year in which it is earned. You will likely conform to a fiscal year ending December 31, unless there is a bona fide non-tax reason to have a non-calendar year end. In that case you can make a special election with Revenue Canada. In the first year of business, you could have a "short year": September 1 to December 31, for example. In that case, you'll need to prorate your deduction for capital cost allowance, and allocate expenses incurred during the time of business only (i.e., mortgage interest, property taxes and other annualized expenses).
Home Office Set-Up	Separate it out from the rest of the house. Measure the square footage of the office and compare this to the total square footage of the living area in the home. Acquire Furniture (Class 8 @ 20% rate), Supplies (100% deductible) and Equipment (Class 8 or Class 10). Keep all receipts for interest, utilities, etc.
Business Vehicle	Convert to business use by finding the Fair Market Value, if the vehicle was previously in use. Or, if new vehicle is acquired, determine the capital cost from the bill of sale. Start keeping a distance log. Save all receipts for operating/fixed costs.
Operations	Classify all expenditures into either capital or operational groupings.
Entertainment Expenses	Mark reason for meeting, name of client on back of all receipts or on invoices. Most of these costs will be restricted to 50% deductibility.
Purchases of Goods for Resale	Keep opening inventory valuations handy, add purchases and deduct closing valuation balances to arrive at Cost of Goods Sold.
Promotional Expenses	100% deductible. Any portion that qualifies for a charitable donation may be written off as a non-refundable tax credit or carried forward.
Communication Costs	Put assets with a useful life of more than one year into CCA classes, do not claim full costs of monthly phone rental unless you have separate business line installed. Long-distance business calls are deductible in full.
Leasing, Equipment Repairs and Maintenance	All deductible in current fiscal year; year end is a good time for maintenance and repairs to reap tax rewards sooner.
Sub-Contracting	Deduct as fees 100%; make sure you can prove this is not really an employer-employee relationship that should have been subject to source deductions.
Salaries, Wages, Bonuses, Vacation Pay	All deductible, as are employer's portions of CPP and EI. Make sure you make source remittances to Revenue Canada on time to avoid penalties.
Professional Fees	Fully deductible in the year incurred, except if on account of capital transactions, in which case they are deductible outlays on Schedule 3.

them and claim a deduction based on a set percentage of the capital cost, as determined by Revenue Canada. Each asset fits into a separate class. In the year of purchase, there is usually a "half-year rule," which means that the capital cost allowance deduction is only available on one-half the acquisition cost. You also need to know that CCA is always taken at the taxpayer's option, so this allows you to do some tax cost averaging over the years.

Auto Expenses   These are also scheduled separately, as we have a two-part task in the tax calculations: first to total all expenses of the year, including operational and fixed costs, and then to prorate these according to the ratio arrived at by taking total business kilometres driven over total kilometres driven in the entire year. To make the calculation an auto log is necessary and will be checked during a tax audit.

Home Office Expenses   These expenses are also prorated for business use; that is the square footage of the workspace, which is exclusively set aside from the living areas of the home, is compared to the total living area and all expenses — interest, property taxes, insurance, utilities, etc. — are totalled and then prorated to get the deductible claim. It is important to know that home workspace expenses cannot be used to increase or create an operating loss. If this happens you'll simply carry forward those unapplied home workspace expenses for use in reducing profits in a future year. The carry-forward is therefore very valuable. Please find information about writing off payments made to family members in Chapter 8.

Partnerships

Partnerships involve a particular form of business organization that differs from a sole proprietorship in several ways. To begin, tax calculations are unique:

- One Statement of Business Activities is prepared for the partnership itself.
- The individual partners, who are allocated a share of the partnership income or losses, attach a copy of the partnership statements to their own returns, and can make an adjustment for individual expenses of the business incurred outside of the partnership.

Therefore, in the case of an unincorporated partnership, it is the individual partners, rather than the partnership, who are subject to tax on the profits or losses of the operation. Partnerships follow the same rules for claiming income and expenses that proprietorships do. (See *Jacks on Tax Savings* and *The Complete Canadian Home Business Guide to Taxes* by Evelyn Jacks for more details.)

In addition, there is a capital component of the partnership that must be recorded and tracked: the interest each partner has in the partnership is considered to be an asset in itself. A taxpayer is considered to have an interest in a partnership when a financial contribution, or equity, is invested. The adjusted cost base of the partnership is increased by equity contributions or any income allocations; it is decreased by equity withdrawals and partnership losses. This must be tracked on an ongoing basis for tax purposes.

Partnership Assets   In general, capital cost allowance is claimed by the partnership on its statements, so assets used should be scheduled by the partnership itself. Certain assets, such as the use of an individual's vehicle can be written off on each individual's income tax return. Capital gains or losses on the disposition of the partnership's assets are calculated by the partnership, and allowances are taken at the partnership level for eligible capital property.

Adjustments for Individual Expenditures   Certain computations must be made at the individual rather than the partnership level:

- Charitable donations and political contributions made by the partnership must be claimed by the individual partner who made them. An adjustment is made to the adjusted cost base of the partnership interest in these cases.
- The individual partner's expenses for advertising, entertainment or expenses for the individual's auto, for example, can be used to reduce the partner's net income from the business on the personal tax return.
- Any GST/HST paid on such income-tax deductible individual expenses qualifies for the GST/HST rebate on Line 457 of the tax return, provided that the partnership is a GST/HST registrant.
- Interest expenses paid on money borrowed to acquire an interest in the partnership or for additional equity contributions must be deducted on a calendar-year basis; other expenses may be deducted either on a calendar year or in the fiscal period ending in a calendar year, depending on the fiscal year end choice made for the business.
- Property that is transferred from an individual to the partnership may be transferred at FMV at the time of transfer, or at certain agreed upon amounts, by special election on Form T2059, *Election on Acquisition of Property by a Canadian Partnership*. However, according to new rules,

where a transferor holds a right to acquire certain non-depreciable capital property whose tax cost is greater than its FMV, within 30 days after disposition, no loss may be recognized on the transfer.

This must be deferred until the earliest of:

- a subsequent disposition of property to a person that is neither the transferor nor a person affiliated with the transferor;
- a change in the property's use from income-producing to non-income producing;
- a "deemed disposition" due to a change of residence or change of taxable status.

Generally speaking, if the partnership acquires the property at less than its capital cost, it is deemed to have acquired it at the capital cost. The partnership is deemed to have taken capital cost allowance equal to the difference.

Be sure you discuss with your tax advisor any transfers of assets from one business organization to another before the transfer, so that you fully understand the tax consequences. This should also hold true when you enter into or leave partnership arrangements.

Partnerships Between Spouses   Where there is a bona fide partnership between spouses, the Attribution Rules should not apply either on the business income or any subsequent capital gain. Each partner would report his or her share of the partnership income and any subsequent gain or loss on disposition of the business, according to their partnership agreements.

However, Revenue Canada can and will adjust the partners' share of income if they are not dealing at arm's length, to an amount the department deems "reasonable" under individual circumstances. This is outlined in the Department's Interpretation Bulletin IT 231R2. Also note that income earned from funds transferred to a limited partner or a partner who is not actively engaged in the partnership will be considered income from "property" rather than business income, which would then be attributable back to the transferor.

To avoid the discretionary power of the Attribution Rules one or all of the following conditions should be met:

- Both spouses are actively engaged in the business (time expended and expertise provided are taken into consideration).
- One spouse is actively engaged in the business, while the other invests his or her property in the business (except as discussed under limited partnerships above).

- Each spouse has invested his or her own property in the business, and the profits or losses are apportioned to these investments.

Before embarking on a family business, it is a good idea to discuss with an accountant or lawyer what form of business organization the venture should take and to draw up specific agreements relating to ownership, remuneration, share of profits, etc. This will not only clarify the effect of attribution rules on your business, but will also help you reap the highest after-tax return for your efforts. At very least, establish firm agreements before starting. This is necessary for tax purposes and is in accordance with prudent business practice. You may wish to:

- Draw up a legal business or partnership agreement between husband and wife showing how annual profits and losses are to be split and how assets are to be shared on terminating the partnership or unincorporated business.
- Itemize which assets will be used in the business.
- Keep separate bank accounts for the business (never mix business funds with personal bank accounts).
- Keep strict and accurate records of all inventory.
- Allocate auto expenses between personal and business use.
- Accurate record-keeping of all income and expenses is essential.

Probably the leading cause of partnership dissolution is the inability for partners to get along. Whether you partner with your spouse, a neighbour, or a colleague, it's most important to document your entry and exit clauses in such a manner so as not to disturb the business enterprise.

Artists and Writers

Tax returns prepared for artists are also unique. The work of artists and writers may require much more time to generate a profit than ordinary businesses. While Revenue Canada had previously taken an aggressive audit stance and disallowed operational losses while the artist establishes profitability, over the years in numerous court cases, the department has consistently lost. The tax department has agreed that continuous losses for many years alone would not be sufficient to establish that there is no reasonable expectation of profit in such ventures.

As a result, a broader application of the tests for profit motive have been established to give direction not only to artists and writers, but other small businesses who need more time to establish profitability. Many of these creative entrepreneurs must also work at other jobs to finance their investment in their businesses in the meantime. Revenue Canada has recognized that other factors must be considered before ruling that the venture is a "hobby" or "sideline" only. Relevant factors include:

- the time devoted to the activity
- the extent to which the taxpayer has exhibited his/her work both in group and private exhibitions or the extent and nature of works published
- the extent to which the taxpayer is represented by private art galleries or art dealers or by publishers or the degree to which bona fide efforts have been made to have works published
- planned or intended course of action, including recent sales of significance, plans for exhibitions, efforts to increase representation by galleries and dealers, recent commissions for work, work in progress, anticipated revenue for royalties and sale of book rights for movies, TV, etc., and receipt of government grants
- the taxpayer's efforts to promote the sale of his/her works
- type of expenditures (i.e., whether a substantial portion of expenses is applicable to research, promotion and direct cost of works or, alternatively, whether the expenses are primarily those that would be expended irrespective of the taxpayer's art activities; for example, office-in-home and auto expenses)
- the increase, if any, in the value of the artist's works as he or she progresses
- the taxpayer's qualifications (i.e., educational background, honours, awards, grants, etc.)
- the significance and growth of gross revenue, as well as the risk of loss
- external factors that may be affecting sales (e.g., economic conditions, change in the public mood, and bankruptcy of art galleries or publishers)
- profit in prior years or continuous losses.

When it comes to claiming specific operational expenses, Revenue Canada has also shown tolerance for the specific circumstances of the artistic community. For example, Revenue Canada has agreed that self-employed performing artists may deduct the cost of music, acting or other lessons to develop their talent. Examples of other deductible expenses for those artists and writers who are self-employed include:

- accounting and legal fees
- agents' commissions
- cost of transportation, including board and lodging if the engagement is out of town, or the costs of transporting a large instrument or equipment
- insurance premiums and repairs to instruments and equipment

- cost of special make-up
- cost of publicity photos
- cost of video-taping or recording performances used for preparation or presentation
- cost of repairs, alterations, and cleaning of clothes used specifically in self-employment
- cost of music, acting or other lessons for a role or part or for general self-improvement in the field
- capital cost allowance on instruments, sheet music, scores, scripts, transcriptions, arrangements, equipment, and wardrobe
- office-in-the-home expenses
- cost of industry-related periodicals
- motor vehicle expenses.

Where an artist is both an employed artist and a self-employed artist for part of the year, expenses must be allocated as follows:

$$\frac{\text{Total Allowable Expenses}}{\text{Total Time Worked}} \times \text{Time Worked as Self-Employed}$$

or any other reasonable allocation.

Visual artists will be allowed to exclude the value of inventory in computing income. Costs will be written off in the year they are incurred rather than apportioning such costs to particular works and claiming them when the works are sold. An artist is also allowed to take a work of art from inventory and, without taking an income inclusion, claim a tax credit for donations if the price qualifies as a certified cultural gift. (See *Jacks on Tax Savings* by Evelyn Jacks for details.)

As well, artists who donate their works to charities may value such a gift at any amount not exceeding its fair market value, but not less than inventory cost. This has the effect of creating income from which the charitable donations can be deducted but may affect other credits.

Artists who receive a project grant that is considered neither as business nor employment income will be allowed to claim such amounts as scholarship income, net of reasonable expenses incurred to fulfil the conditions of the grant, and also net of the $500 scholarship exemption. However, the value of workshops, seminars and other training programs provided to an artist who belongs to a national arts service organization will be taxable.

Child Care Providers

This business profile is also an interesting one, because it sets an example for the self-employed who may have a number of otherwise personal expenditures that have a primarily business component. We are speaking here of the claim for home workspace, food and toy costs.

A self-employed baby-sitter may deduct various business expenses against income earned from the baby-sitting enterprise, including government grants. To report income earned and deductible expenses on the tax return, the self-employed baby-sitter must keep a record of all income received; therefore, a separate bank account for such deposits would be a good idea. Like other small business owners, she should begin keeping receipts of items purchased and used in the baby-sitting business.

The dilemma often faced is this: "I use my whole home for the business when the children are here. How do I properly allocate the personal portion?" If there is no one area set aside exclusively for the business, portions of rent, mortgage interest, property taxes, utilities and repairs would be deductible, according to the amount of floor space used in the baby-sitting business and *the number of hours the daycare centre is open,* as illustrated below:

$$\text{Total Operating Expenses of the home} \times \frac{\text{Square footage of home workspace}}{\text{Total square footage}} \times \frac{\text{No. of hours daycare is open in the year}}{\text{Total hours in the year}}$$

The result of this equation is the total deductible home workspace expenses. These claims must follow normal rules; that is, home workspace costs must not increase or create a loss.

Additional deductions for food, toys and supplies related to the business would also be deductible. As well, a claim for capital cost allowance could be made for assets such as furniture, office equipment or a vehicle used in the enterprise.

Deductible Child Care Expenses:

- Accounting Costs
- Advertising
- Art & Craft Supplies
- Auto Expenses
- Bank Charges
- Blankets
- Books
- Capital Cost Allowances
- Diapers
- Employee Expenses
- Entrance Fees to Parks, etc.
- Cost of Field Trips
- Food
- Household Costs
- Insurance
- Postage
- Repairs
- Soap and Shampoo
- Telephone/Communications*
- Towels and Toothbrushes
- Toys for the Children
- Training Courses
- Travel Costs**

* Note, unless a separate business line is installed, the monthly rental on the personal phone will not be deductible.

** Per trip expenses may be claimed instead of keeping a detailed auto log if you only use a vehicle occasionally for business purposes.

Food costs, may prove to be a problem to track. If all food consumed by the children could be purchased separately, the full food bills could be deducted. However, in most cases, food is purchased at the same time for both family and business consumption. Therefore, in a separate book of account, the baby-sitter should keep a record of food items to feed the children and then prorate the total food bill accordingly.

Once all the applicable deductions are taken from baby-sitting income, it is possible that the baby-sitter's net income, which is used in computing the Spousal Amount, is low enough for a full or partial claim by the higher-earning spouse. If net income is just over the threshold limits, a Registered Retirement Savings Plan could be purchased for the self-employed spouse, if she reported earned income last year. The results would be a greatly reduced net income, resulting in a possible Spousal Amount Claim for the higher-income earner, and possibly increased refundable tax credits such as the Canada Child Tax Benefit.

Like other self-employed persons, the baby-sitter can begin making contributions on her own behalf to the Canada Pension Plan based on net income from her business.

When issuing receipts, the baby-sitter should break down how much money the parents paid for children under seven and those over six, so that parents can take advantage of higher allowable deduction limits for preschoolers.

Farmers

The income from farming is considered to be business income that is subject to the same tax-filing provisions applicable to other businesses. That is, a Statement of Business Activities must be filed with the tax return. Farmers who are not NISA (Net Income Stabilization Account) participants will use Form T2042, *Statement of Farming Income and Expenses*, to report income and expenses from farming activities. Those who are NISA participants will use Form T1163 or sometimes T1164.

Most of us think of farmers as those who raise cattle or other domestic animals, or as those who grow grain. However, other activities that are considered "farming enterprises" include the tillage of soil, maintenance of race horses, bee-keeping, operation of a wild game reserve, nursery or greenhouse businesses, fruit growing, raising poultry, fur farming, growing Christmas trees or even raising fish. Here's what you need to know to make sure your offsetting expenses are deductible:

Filing Methods   Persons who are in the business of farming or fishing may use the cash method of accounting to compute their income. This method calculates income actually received during the year that is reduced by expenses actually paid during the year. They also have the option of reporting income using the accrual method; income is calculated as it becomes receivable and expenses are deducted as they become payable.

The farmer may elect to use the cash method by filing a tax return using the cash method. Once this is done, all subsequent returns must be filed in a similar manner, and a formal request to change must be made to the Director of the local Tax Services Office. In the case of a partnership, each partner must elect to have the income from the farming or fishing business reported using the cash method. This means that all partners must file a tax return in the year of election.

Instalment Payments Farmers are required to remit tax in instalments, but only once a year, on or before December 31, based on two-thirds of estimated tax for the current year. Canada Pension Plan contributions are also required on net farming income and should be factored into the instalment payments.

Reporting Farm Expenses Farm expenses are reported on Form T2042/T1164, and can include the following:

- building and fence repairs
- capital cost allowance on assets owned, claimed at your option
- cleaning, levelling and draining land
- crop insurance, GRIP and stabilization premiums, as well as NISA administration fees
- interest on farm loans, mortgages and vehicles
- insurance on farm buildings, and in certain cases, life insurance policy premiums (that is, only if the policy was used as collateral for a business loan. For more details, see IT 309)
- machinery expenses including gas, diesel fuel and oil, repairs, licences and insurance
- mandatory inventory adjustments included in income last year
- memberships and subscription fees
- motor vehicle costs, prorated for any personal-use component
- livestock purchased
- professional fees
- property taxes
- office supply costs
- optional inventory adjustments included in income last year
- rent for land buildings or pastures
- salaries, wages and benefits, including employer's contributions, for family members (also see page 100)

- small tools that cost less than $200
- utility bills for farm buildings
- seeds, plants, feed, supplements, straw and bedding, pesticides, veterinary fees and breeding fees
- 50% of meals and entertainment costs.

Home Workspace Expenses   Certain household expenses can be claimed as a business expense on the tax return under the general provisions for home workspace expenses. This includes heat, electricity, insurance, maintenance, mortgage interest, property taxes and other expenses, prorated for the business/personal-use portions and subject to the restrictions that no loss can be increased or created using the home office expenses.

Telephone Bills   Long-distance calls that are personal in nature may not be deducted. Circle all personal calls on every monthly phone bill and use the rest of the bill as a deduction, if you have a separate business phone. If there is no separate phone, the monthly rental charge is usually considered a personal expense.

Deductible Wages for Spouse   Salaries paid to a spouse or common law spouse in a family business are fully deductible, provided the following factors are in place:

- the work was required to be done, was actually done and would otherwise have required the hiring of a stranger
- wages were reasonable and actually paid and documented.

All persons employed by spouses must have Employment Insurance Premiums withheld and remitted, as well as Canada Pension Plan premiums and Income Taxes. A T4 Slip must be issued under normal rules. Employment by a person who controls 40% or more of the issued voting shares is not insurable; neither is employment of a spouse unless the remuneration is tax deductible under the Income Tax Act (see comments below), nor is a salary level that is unreasonably high. These tax provisions can make a considerable impact on the incomes of farmers and owners of small businesses. In effect, both spouses can earn income in their own right, allowing for legitimate income splitting within the family.

Wages Paid to Children   The same general rules apply to children's wages (that is, reasonable wages must be actually paid for services that were necessary in producing income and that would have required the services of outside help). The employer must also contribute a portion of the premiums paid by the child to the Employment Insurance Commission (or Canada Pension Plan if child is 18 or over) on the source deductions remittance form. The employer's portion is a deductible expense.

There are some important points to remember when paying your children:

- If you pay your children by cheque, the tax department will accept your cancelled cheque as a legitimate receipt.
- Receipts signed by the child are required if you pay cash.
- If you give your child livestock or grain in lieu of money for the payment of wages, the child must report the value of this livestock or grain on his/her tax return as income. In order to claim the wage expenses, you will be required to include in your gross sales income the value of this property given to your child.
- The value of board may not be claimed as an expense if this is supplied to any child who is dependent upon you for support.

Source Deduction Remittances for Small Business   Those employers with average monthly withholding amounts of less than $1,000 for the second preceding calendar year, and who have no compliance problems in either their withholding account or GST/HST account, for the preceding 12 months may choose to remit their source deductions withheld from employees on a quarterly rather than a monthly basis. These remittances would be required on March 31, June 30, September 30 and December 31. The remittances are due the 15th of the month following the end of each quarter.

Vehicle Costs   The most important part of claiming any vehicle expenses is to keep a distance log, which can record your total business driving for the year, if your vehicle was used both for personal and business driving. To make a claim on your return, you will need to know the Total Business Kilometres driven and divide that by the Total Kilometres driven in the year. The size of deductible expenditures for your vehicles depends on how many you have and what they are used for. Restrictions on certain expenses apply to passenger vehicles.

Farm trucks or vans, on the other hand, are "motor vehicles" that will be exempt from these restrictions if they are designed to carry the driver and two passengers and are used primarily (which means more than 50% of the time) to transport equipment or goods, or if the motor vehicle is used 90% or more of the time to transfer equipment, goods or passengers for the purpose of earning income.

Group receipts in categories before you compute deductible totals. All of the following expenses are deductible: gas and oil; interest on loans (subject to restrictions for passenger vehicles); insurance; licence renewal costs; tires and repairs; lease payments (again, restrictions may apply to passenger vehicles); auto club premiums; car washes; parking and tolls. By keeping all receipts in order and faithfully maintaining a distance log, you will maximize your tax deductions and minimize the time required to file your tax return. Joint owners of a motor vehicle cannot deduct more than one owner could deduct.

Ineligible Expenses   Expenses not allowable include:

- replacement or improvement of assets (these must be capitalized)
- principal payments on borrowed money, including repayments of a loan for tile drainage
- the value of animals that have died during the year (when they are purchased, the cost is written off as an expense)
- expenses for a personal garden or upkeep of livestock gifted to children.

Inventory Valuations   To combat the fluctuations in income that a farmer may experience, the role of his/her inventory is an important one in determining the net income each year. That is because Revenue Canada wishes to avoid tax loss reporting in cases where expenditures have been made to increase inventory size. There are two inventory provisions for the farmer. One is optional, the other mandatory.

MIA   Revenue Canada won't just let you write off operational losses from a farm, if you have purchased inventory on hand. A Mandatory Inventory Adjustment must be made. The effect of this provision is to reduce the amount of the cash loss a farmer may have in one tax year, by adding in the value of inventory on hand at year end. Valuation of inventory costs is at the lesser of cash cost or FMV. Amounts included in income must be deducted the following year, thereby reducing income earned from operations in that year.

OIA   Under the cash method, a farmer has a further opportunity to average income and losses over the years, by electing to make an Optional Inventory Adjustment. Such an adjustment, which adds the Fair Market Value of all remaining inventory not used in the MIA provision to a farmer's income, will further reduce a farmer's remaining cash loss in one year, and then be deducted from income the next. The definition of inventory for these purposes may include all inventory on hand including livestock owned, cash crops, fertilizer, chemicals, feed, seed, fuel, etc. Proper management of this provision can save the farmer thousands of dollars over the years.

Certain Prepayments   Under the cash method of reporting income, amounts are generally deducted when paid. However, a deduction for prepaid expenses can be made in advance, but only for the current year and one more year. The portion of amounts paid for tax years that are two or more years after the actual payment must be deferred and deducted in those future years.

For example, if $5,000 was prepaid for five consecutive years of insurance coverage, $2,000 could be deducted in 1995 and then $1,000 in each year 1997, 1998 and 1999.

To be deductible, the amount is required to have been paid in a preceding tax year and cannot be deductible in computing income of the business for any other year.

Land Improvement Costs   Expenditures, such as clearing land and constructing unpaved roads, are deducted as a current expense by farmers. A farmer may claim less than the full cost of these expenses in the year they are incurred. He or she will be allowed to carry forward and use the remaining undeducted amounts in a subsequent year. This is significant to farmers who have little or no net income in the year the expenditure is made, because it allows the deferral of the write-off to a year when there is taxable income. As well, the cost of laying or installing a land drainage system will be deductible, whether it is composed of tile or other materials.

Livestock Income Tax-Deferral Program   Here's a little known tax saver. A tax-deferral program exists for farmers who had to deplete their breeding herds of grazing livestock because of drought conditions. Farmers will be required to include the proceeds received for the forced destruction or sale of breeding animals in income. However, an offsetting deduction may be taken to defer tax on such proceeds to the next tax year. Qualifying areas will be determined every year upon recommendation by the Minister of Agriculture and Agri-Food. Ask your tax advisor to brief you on this year's prescribed areas.

Restricted Farm Losses   Farmers whose chief source of income is not from farming are currently restricted to a maximum farm loss write-off of $2,500 plus one-half of the next $12,500 for a maximum of $8,750. This means that a loss of $15,000 or more will qualify for a write-off of $8,750.

This provision of the Act is the subject of numerous court cases. Farmers argue that they are in the full time business of farming and therefore should be allowed full loss deductibility; while Revenue Canada argues that the chief source of income is not from farming and therefore losses should be restricted. Under current rules, Revenue Canada groups farm losses into three categories:

* Losses from a full-scale farming operation (the taxpayer spends all of his/her time and effort in the operation of the farm and farming is the chief source of income). These losses are deductible in full against other income the taxpayer may have.
* Farm losses claimed against other income when it is clear that the taxpayer's chief source of income is not farming.
* Farm losses claimed against other income when it is questionable whether a business actually exists. (These losses are not deductible at all, because the activities are considered to be a hobby.)

The tax department will look at a number of conditions as proof that a viable operation exists. These guidelines are also useful in determining whether other business ventures have a reasonable expectation of profit:

Gross and Net Income From the Farming Operation   This includes the amount of capital invested, and a close look at the cash flow of the business.

* **The Size of the Property Used for Farming**. Your losses may be disallowed if:
  * Your property is too small to project any hope of profit.
  * You have made no attempt at farming or developing your land.
  * You have no intention of using more than a fraction of the land over a period of years. There must be potential for profit that you can document and justify with cash flow statements and budgets for the future.

* **Qualifications of the Taxpayer.** Losses will generally be allowed if:
  * You have farming background experience and spend most of your time on the operation during the busy months.
  * You make commitments for the future expansion of the farm.
  * You qualify for some type of provincial assistance.
  * You personally are involved to a large degree in the operations.

- **Other Sources of Income**. Generally speaking, if your chief source of income is from other sources, losses may be restricted or disallowed. If forced to earn income elsewhere in a bad year, full losses may be allowed if it can be proven that farming is still your chief source of income and that it is your intention to continue spending most of your time and money on the future of the farm.
- **Future Business Plans**. Be prepared to show how your farm will be maintained and developed in future years.

Also be aware that if you have a capital gain, perhaps from farmland sold during the year, interest or property taxes that were included in any restricted farm losses of prior years that have not yet been deducted may be used to reduce the capital gain, but not to create or increase a capital loss on the sale of the farmland.

Value of Accounts Receivable   Effective July 13, 1990, a taxpayer is required to include the value of accounts receivable in income in cases where (1) a Canadian resident ceases to carry on the business of farming and becomes a non-resident; (2) a Canadian resident ceases to carry on a farming business in another country and becomes a non-resident; and (3) a non-resident ceases to carry on a Canadian farming business after July 13, 1990. In such cases, inventory will be considered disposed of at its fair market value.

Farmers and the GST/HST   Most farmers should enquire about becoming GST/HST registrants when speaking to their accountants, or to Revenue Canada directly. This is because most supplies produced by farmers are zero-rated; that is, no GST/HST is charged by the farmer on the sale of supplies, but a GST/HST input tax credit can be claimed. This amounts to a recovery of GST/HST paid on purchases incurred in producing supplies. Examples of zero-rated supplies are livestock used to produce wool or food, grains, seeds (not garden seeds) and fodder crops, share cropping and unprocessed fish.

Special Capital Cost Allowances Classes and Rates for Farmers   Most items of farm equipment can be considered as depreciable assets, subject to a variety of prescribed classes and rates. Generally, they fall into Class 8/20% for non-motorized equipment, and Class 10/30% for motorized equipment or computer equipment.

For a complete list, see Revenue Canada's Farming Income Guide. Farmers who buy certain pollution-control manure-handling equipment, including pads, liquid manure tanks, pumps and spreaders may qualify for special accelerated CCA rates. Contact the Minister of the Environment for more details.

Also note that the cost of paving roads must be added to Class 17, which has an 8% rate. Casing and cribwork for a waterwell as well as the cost of the system that distributes water, such as the pump, pipes and trenches, will all be capitalized in Class 8, which has a 20% rate.

Eligible Capital Properties   Farmers who own milk and egg quotas have what is known as an "eligible capital property," which is a property that has a lasting economic value and therefore must be written off over time. To do so, a special account is set up — the cumulative eligible capital account — and 3/4 of the value of the quota is recorded here. The annual allowance that is claimed against other income is 7% of this amount. However, a CEC allowance deduction will only be allowed if there is a positive balance in the account. A negative balance would have to be reported as income. If the property is qualified farm property eligible for the $500,000 Capital Gains Exemption, qualifying income amounts will be reported on Schedule 3 Capital Gains and Losses, to enable the deduction.

New Rules on Capital Gains Exemption   The February 22, 1994, federal budget may have eliminated the $100,000 Capital Gains Exemption for gains realized on capital property after budget day. However, the Super Exemption — $500,000 on the disposition of small business shares and qualified farm property — will remain untouched and available, for now at least.

The Super Exemption may be used on the gains generated by the disposal of shares of the capital stock of a small business corporation owned by the individual or partnership related to him or her. A small business corporation is a Canadian-controlled private corporation in which all or substantially all of the assets are used in an active business carried on primarily in Canada. The shares must be owned by such an individual through the 24 months immediately prior to the disposition. During the holding period, more than 50% of the FMV of the corporation's assets must have been used in an active business.

Qualifying farm property, on the other hand, refers to farm property acquired after June 17, 1987, including real property owned by the taxpayer, spouse or child for at least 24 months immediately before sale. A gross revenue test must be met; that is, in at least two years prior to disposition, gross income earned by the individual by active farming operations, must exceed net income from all other sources. Second, all or substantially all of the fair value of the farm assets must be used in active business operations for at least 24 months prior to disposition.

On farms acquired before June 17, 1987, the Super Exemption will be allowed if the farmland and buildings were used in an active farming business in Canada in the year of sale, and at least five years prior to the disposition.

Consult your tax advisor about meeting the qualifications to enable a future tax-free gain of farming property held by your family.

Family Farm Rollovers When a farmer dies, a tax-free rollover of farm assets, including the farmland, depreciable properties and eligible capital properties, will be allowed on transfers to the spouse, children or grandchildren. This means that no capital gain or loss or terminal loss or recapture will generally arise on the tax return of the deceased. However, to qualify, the property must have been used principally in an active farming business.

The meaning of "child" has been extended to include persons who, before reaching age 19, were under the control and custody of the taxpayer and dependent upon him. This could include nephews, nieces and in-laws. The cost of acquisition of the property is equal to the deceased's deemed proceeds of disposition.

As well, farm rollovers from a child to a parent would be allowed in cases in which the child dies leaving a surviving parent.

Property eligible for such transfers includes property leased by a taxpayer to the family farm corporation. A special election is available to transfer depreciable property on death (including buildings, equipment or other depreciable property used in business). This may be done in any amount between the fair market value of the property and its undepreciated capital cost at the time of transfer. Eligible capital property (ECP) can be transferred at any amount between FMV and:

$$4/3 \times \text{Cumulative Eligible Capital} \quad \times \quad \frac{\text{FMV of Property}}{\text{FMV of all Eligible Capital Property}}$$

Other capital property, such as land, may be transferred at any amount between the fair market value and the adjusted cost base immediately prior to death, as summarized in Figure 7.2:

Figure 7.2	Transfer of Farm Assets

Asset	While Living	At Death		Transfers to Spouse or Child
Equipment	At any amount between FMV and transferor's undepreciated capital cost	$\dfrac{\text{FMV of asset}}{\substack{\text{FMV of all}\\\text{assets in}\\\text{that class}}} \times$	UCC of all assets in that class	Special Election: The lower of Capital Cost Or Capital Cost of all property in same class $\times$ UCC of all in same class Or FMV if transferred to spouse, Or an amount between FMV and special election for transfer to child
Land	At an amount between the fair market value and the transferor's ACB	At the adjusted cost base immediately before death, or any amount between ACB and FMV		

Note: The deceased's legal representative may choose to transfer property at any amount between its FMV and ACB or UCC before death. In the case of the spouse, the property must have vested indefeasibly in the spouse within 36 months of date of death.

Recent clarification to the tax-deferred rollover rules on inter-generational transfers of certain farm property, including depreciable property, from a taxpayer to a child, ensures that proceeds of disposition can be treated as being equal to the lesser of the capital cost and the cost amount to the taxpayer immediately before death, as illustrated above. Also, a tax-free rollover of the deceased's Net Income Stabilization Account Fund No. 2 is allowed, together with a tax-filing extension to 18 months of a deceased's final return.

Careful planning of cost values would allow the farmer to use the capital gains exemption on transfer and would increase the acquisition cost to the spouse or child, so as to affect the tax burden these dependants may have sometime in the future when the property is disposed of. The key is to build a tax-efficient legacy well in advance of making a decision about a disposition.

Note: A farmer who transfers shares of a family farm corporation or interests in a family farm partnership at fair market value to his/her child who then disposes of it before attaining age 18 will be subject to the attribution rules on farm income earned. The same attribution rules would hold true in cases where a spouse disposes of the property during the farmer's lifetime except this time attribution applies to the capital gain or loss.

THE TAX ADVISOR

There are two documents you should produce and discuss with your tax advisors during the year. The first is a **Tax Action Planner,** which records tax-filing milestones throughout the year on your Daily Business Journal. It might be summarized as in Figure 7.3.

The second document you should keep is a **Taxfiler Profile Folder.** This is particularly important in families with a variety of business enterprises, who are in a good position to do some tax cost averaging. It is most important for these families to file their income tax returns together and to maximize their tax-filing opportunities. An individual planner should be set up for each member of the family. This will help you visualize tax-filing profiles of each person as they emerge during the year, and give you a good starting point in your discussions with your tax advisor. You'll be able to use your time wisely, ask better questions, and to focus on your issues of concern, because you have the information summarized and at your fingertips. A good example appears in *Jacks on Tax Savings* by Evelyn Jacks. However, small business owners should also include a business profile overview, similar to the one shown in Figure 7.4.

Figure 7.3	Tax Action Planner				
Month	**Week 1**	**Week 2**	**Week 3: 15th**	**Week 4**	**Week 5: 30th**
January	RRSP contr. Mo. end review	Payroll Accts. Payable	Remit Source Deductions, GST for Dec.	Payroll	Final Quarter Review
February	RRSP Contr. Overview T4s, T5s, T3s Mo. end review	Payroll Accts. Payable	Remit Source Deductions, Prepare to remit tax return	Payroll, Mail or Distribute T4 Slips	
March	RRSP Contr. Mo. end review	Payroll, Accts. Payable	Remit Source Deductions, Instalments	Payroll	**Appointment with Tax Advisor re tax return**
April	RRSP Contr. Mo. End review	Payroll, Accts. Payable	Remit Source Deductions, GST for 1st quarter	Payroll	lst Quarter **Review; File tax return if you owe money**

Continue planner for the months of May through December

Figure 7.4   Business Profile Overview

Business Name: _____

Type Of Business:

Proprietorship   Owner: _____

Partnership   Partners: _____

_____

_____

Corporation _____ Date of Incorporation _____ Costs: _____

Business Plan:

Source of Revenue:	Year 1	Year 2	Year 3	Year 4	Year 5
Total					

Operating Expenses:	Year 1	Year 2	Year 3	Year 4	Year 5
Total					
% Of Income					

Profits	Year 1	Year 2	Year 3	Year 4	Year 5
Total					
% Of Income					

Obstacles Forecast: _____

_____

_____

_____

RECAP: 8 Easy Steps to Profile for Profitability

1. **Know your Tax-Filing Profile.** Know what business you're in and get ready to communicate this to your tax advisor. Set up at least two formal meetings, one in March and one in November, to discuss your tax savings options. A meeting in August or September will help you decide whether you wish to request a change in your instalment remittances. Then prepare the **Taxfilers Profile Folder** to get ready for tax-filing season, all year long.

2. **Choose the right method of reporting income.** Make sure you choose the correct reporting method when you start your business, and that you know the exceptions to the rules. Farmers and very small businesses may use the "cash method" of reporting income, for example. That is, income is reported when it is actually received, while expenses are reported when they are actually paid. Most other businesses, though, must report their income on the "accrual basis." In that case, income is reported when it is earned and expenses deducted when they are incurred. Special provisions may be available for certain professionals, farmers, and those who qualify for a variety of reserving provisions. Discuss this concept with your tax advisor.

3. **Plan the deduction of operating expenses.** Save every receipt and invoice and mark each document to tell a story: why you made the expenditure, who you entertained, purpose of the meeting, etc. This will help you prove "reasonable expectation" in a tax audit in the future. Remember that operating expenses are 100% deductible against revenues of the business. In the case of husband and wife teams, it is most important to show that personal living expenses are not claimed against business income.

4. **Plan to write off tax losses.** If expenses exceed revenues, a non-capital loss results. In general, this loss can be used to offset other income of the current year first; if there is an excess loss, it can be either carried back three years to offset other income in those years, or carried forward for a period of seven years (ten years in the case of farmers). Should you have an operating loss, you may wish to save certain optional deductions for the future, like your capital cost allowance deduction, your interest deduction on depreciable assets, which can be capitalized, or your RRSP deduction. However, Revenue Canada has made a practice of scrutinizing certain industries more thoroughly than others when it comes to writing off tax losses. This is particularly true of the farming community and the construction industry. Discuss the loss-filing rules applicable to your industry with your tax advisor.

5. **Know how to maximize the computation of capital cost allowances.** CCA is always taken at the taxpayer's option. Claiming CCA differs with individual businesses, as asset types and classes will change. Ask your tax advisor about the write-offs available for your proposed asset purchases, and what special tax provisions might be available for your industry. Robes of judges and lawyers may be depreciated in Class 8 for example; certain entertainers costumes can be depreciated there as well; otherwise street clothes are not deductible.

6. **Disposition of assets can result in tax consequences.** Should all the assets in a particular class be sold or otherwise disposed of, at an amount less than the Undepreciated Capital Cost, a "terminal loss" may be written off against other business income of the year. Should the opposite happen, "recapture" of deductions previously taken will be added to income, but only up to the original cost of the assets. Should you dispose of the asset for an amount higher than the original cost, you'll report a capital gain on Schedule 3. Asset-intensive business profiles, like farmers, will want to take note of these in their decision-making processes.

7. **Computation of auto expenses.** Rule #1, keep the distance log. Rule #2, find out if your business vehicle is subject to the passenger vehicle restrictions. Rule #3, partners generally claim for auto expenses as an adjustment to the partnership business activities statement, and qualify for a GST/HST rebate if the partnership is registered. Make sure you know the rules as they pertain to your business vehicles.

8. **Compute home workspace costs.** Every home-based business owner must calculate these costs separately, as a special proration must be done to allocate costs only to the business portion of the home. Make sure you have all the bills, the sketch of the workspace and prepare the calculation each and every year. You may not create or increase a business loss with a claim for home office expenses, so schedule the costs and carry them forward from year to year in those cases. Some businesses will claim for an office space only; others will have a manufacturing space and possibly a storage space. Be sure you can show Revenue Canada why your business profile deserves to claim the space you use.

9. **Make personal-use adjustments.** Self-employed taxpayers can really increase their tax deductions — legitimately — by making a list of all personal expenditures that have a business component, and then claiming a portion of the costs. However, certain business profiles are

subject to greater scrutiny than others. Farmers should always be prepared to adjust for any expense items that were used personally — livestock consumed by the family, for example, if the cost was written off as an expense. The same rule holds true for cosmetics and cleaning products sales representatives. Remember, every dollar counts towards tax savings, so be sure to make a claim for partial business use, where valid. But always add back any personal use component of any items so used and written off in your business statements.

10. **Know why you could be chosen for audit.** Revenue Canada audits those who do not keep adequate books, do not file returns, don't register for the GST/HST. Revenue Canada has profiled certain industries due to their work with Statistics Canada, who have identified the skimming of receipts by certain small businesses as a major component of the Underground Economy. Since 1996 Revenue Canada has identified over 220,000 business non-filers and over 11,000 GST/HST non-filers (as per *Compliance: From Vision to Strategy*). Special investigative projects have been identified in the following areas:

    - independent couriers
    - subcontractors in construction and home building
    - unregistered car salespeople
    - carpet installers
    - direct sellers
    - mechanics
    - auto body repairers

    If you are in a high-risk group, be sure to put your affairs in order, as the probability of audit is higher in those identified industries.

CHAPTER 8

How to Put Your Family to Work and Write it Off!

"See it big, and keep it simple."
WILFRED PETERSON

KEY CONCEPTS

- You can hire your family members to work in your business and write off the cost of their wages
- To be deductible, amounts must be paid for work actually performed
- The amounts paid must be reasonable, and in line with what a stranger would have been paid
- The amounts must be incurred in pursuit of profits from the business
- RRSP contributions should be encouraged for all family members, together with the filing of a return.

REAL LIFE: Raj and his wife Vasi were happy to live in Canada. They had immigrated from their native India last year, and in January of the new year opened their own business in Canada—an Indian restaurant. Vasi did the cooking, with her sous-chef, daughter Tara, while Raj and his son Ram, played host and waiter respectively. After their first quarter in business, their books showed a small operating profit. However, the proprietorship showed no deductions for wages for the family members, and Raj wondered if he could reduce his tax liability any further by paying his family members. Was this possible? How would he justify payment of wages and the work of the family retroactively?

THE PROBLEM

Most new businesses in Canada have something in common: usually the whole family pitches in to get the business established profitably. While it is legally possible to pay your family members to work in your small business, and deduct the amounts from the profits of your business, be careful not to make the common mistake that Raj has made: he didn't keep the documentation required to show that the family members were actually working in the business, and, worse, he didn't actually pay them the money. Therefore at tax time, he'll be unable to write off any salary or wage expenses retroactively. However, for the future, Raj and his family are poised for some significant tax savings solutions.

THE SOLUTION

Family members can be hired as hourly employees, wage earners, sub-contractors, commission salespeople, or any other position you would hire a stranger for. You can pay them salary, wages, gratuities, overtime, premium hours, banked time, retroactive earnings, salary, bonuses, commissions, advances, draws, gifts, severance, sick leave, vacation pay, wages in lieu of notice or a number of taxable or tax-free benefits.

However a simple rule must be followed in hiring and remunerating your family members: *treat the process of hiring and paying your family members in the same manner as if you were hiring a stranger.* All the paperwork must be in place, including the signing of employment contracts or sub-contracts, or the keeping of time cards to support hours worked. Without the paperwork, not only will it be impossible to write off the amounts paid to your family members, but you'll also miss out on an important tax saver: the ability to legitimately split income amongst family members.

The establishment of formal payroll records, however, can only happen once your have determined whether you have an employer-employee relationship with your family members who work in your business. If you do, certain statutory source deductions must be made from gross pay and remitted to the government on a regular basis.

You should also know that there are a number of important tax-savings tips that you can utilize in designing compensation packages for your employees, including family members. For example, you should always be conscious of the **Cardinal Rule of Employment Contracts:**

Put as many after-tax dollars in your employee's pockets, as soon as possible. There are many ways to do this, including the minimization of taxes withheld at source.

THE PARAMETERS

The following parameters should be observed in order to deduct amounts paid to family members for working in your small business:

Formalize Hiring Practices

When a business hires an employee, generally the employee is given a job description, a rate of pay or salary level, and a series of expectations that can include termination, confidentiality and non-compete clauses. When a business hires a sub-contractor, the self-employed person generally submits a proposal to the business to perform a certain task that has a start and end period and an agreed-upon invoice price.

In a family business, such formalities are often dropped or forgotten about. However, they are just as important, and certainly, from a tax point of view, even more important, as Revenue Canada will scrutinize these "non-arm's length" transactions even more closely. (A non-arm's length relationship generally exists when one deals with someone related by blood, marriage or adoption.)

To legitimize your deduction for amounts paid to family members, Revenue Canada will want to know that the following criteria are met:

- The work actually has to have been done by your relative
- The work was necessary and would have otherwise required the hiring of a stranger
- The amounts paid compared to what would have been paid to a stranger for the same work
- The amounts paid were reasonable in relation to the relative's age and experience
- The amounts were paid in pursuit of profits from the business.

It is a very good idea to establish a Human Resource Guide or Policies and Procedures Manual in which your human resource policies are outlined. This can include things like job descriptions, job postings, employer-paid training, sick leave and vacation policies, sexual harassment and bereavement policies, and so on. This will also show to Revenue Canada that you are running a serious, for-profit business with a future orientation for earning profits.

Employed or Self-Employed?

This is an important question, as the business owner will have certain obligations to meet by law, if the relationship is one of "master-servant":

• Revenue Canada defines an employer-employee relationship as follows:

"a verbal or written agreement in which an employee agrees to work on a full-time or part-time basis for a specified or indeterminate period of time, in return for salary or wages. The employer has the right to decide where, when and how the work will be done. In this type of relationship a *contract of service* exists."*

When a family member works in the business, the owner must do the following:

• Make statutory deductions from gross pay contribution to the Canada Pension Plan, Employment Insurance and Income Taxes. These must be remitted usually once a month, although very small businesses have the option to remit each quarter. Children under 18 need not contribute to the Canada Pension Plan; while those over 70 or in receipt of CPP benefits need not contribute at all.

• Prepare a T4 slip for each employee and issue it by the end of February each year.

Where a family member works as a subcontractor to the business, a "business relationship" is said to exist. Revenue Canada defines a business relationship to be the following:

"a verbal or written agreement in which a self-employed individual agrees to perform specific work for a payer in return for payment. There is no employer or employee. The self-employed individual generally does not have to carry out all or even part of the work himself. In this type of relationship, a *contract for service* exists."*

The amounts invoiced to the business must be paid in a timely fashion to the sub-contractor, (usually within 30 days). By the way, the invoiced amount is fully deductible by the business owner.

The subcontractor who is unincorporated must then remit CPP premiums via the income tax return at year end, and in some cases, tax instalment payments, quarterly.

In addition, if the subcontractor earns more than $30,000 in gross fees billed, GST/HST registration may be required. This should be

* Revenue Canada publication: *Employee or Self-Employed?*

taken into consideration before deciding on what status your family member prefers to have in working within your business.

Therefore, you will need to know whether the relationship you have is a contract *of* service or a contract *for* service. There are four basic factors Revenue Canada will look at if the determination is borderline:

1. **Control.** The degree of control exercised by the payer will help to define the relationship with the person doing the work. If the payer has the right to hire or fire, controls the payments of wages and how much is to be paid, and decides on the time, place and manner in which the work should be done, including hours of work, and the assessment of quality of work, generally there is a strong indication of an employer-employee relationship. Additional factors include control of the list of clients of the business and the territory covered, as well as training and development.

2. **Ownership of Assets and Tools.** If the payer supplies the equipment and tools required to perform the tasks of the job and pays for repairs, insurance, rental, fuel or other costs of operation, generally an employer-employee relationship is considered to exist.

3. **Risk of Loss.** The payer is generally considered to be the employer if s/he assumes the financial risk for the company including the responsibility for covering operating costs like office expenses, salaries, insurance coverage, freight and delivery, rent, bad debts, damage and promotional expenses. Those who receive remuneration without financial risk—that is salary is paid in full regardless of the health of the business—would generally be considered to be an employee.

4. **Integration.** This final factor is considered from the worker's viewpoint. If the worker is not dependent on the payer, and simply integrates the job done for the payer into his own business activities, the worker is likely self-employed. It would be important to show that the self-employed person has other jobs lined up with other suppliers, for example, to consolidate this position. However, if the job done for the payer is actually integrated into the payer's commercial activities, to the extent that the worker is connected with the employer's business and dependent on it, likely an employer-employee relationship exists.

Taken all together, the circumstances surrounding these four criteria will generally help you to determine whether an employer-employee relationship exists.

REAL LIFE: Marina works in her husband Paul's construction business, doing the books. She has a home office, she answers the phone for the business from there and prepares the books on the computer that Paul bought
for her. He has asked her to be in the office available for calls from 9 until 2
every day, but Marina often spends all day there to finish correspondence,
invoicing and other odds and ends. Paul is her only payer.

In this case there is a very strong likelihood that Marina will be considered to be Paul's employee. He has acquired and written off the
equipment she needs to do her job; he controls the place and the time
she works and she has no other clients. She should be filling in a time
card to post her hours worked; or he should have Marina on an employment contract if salary is being paid. He should issue a T4 slip at year
end, and make periodic source remittances for CPP, EI and Income Tax.

If Paul was one of a series of clients for whom Marina was doing the
books, if she purchased her own equipment and tools, if it could be
shown that Marina took on the risk of paying overhead and responsibility for the contracts she bid and won, there would be an indication that
Marina, in fact, was self-employed. Marina would then become a supplier
of Paul's and submit invoices to be paid within usually a 30-day period.

In that case, Marina would have to do at least four things from Revenue Canada's perspective:

- self-report her income on her income tax return
- make CPP premium contributions via the tax return at the end of
  the tax year when she files her return
- pay tax instalment payments if she owed Revenue Canada more
  than $2,000 in the current tax year and the immediately preceding
  year and
- register to collect the GST/HST if her gross earnings exceeded
  $30,000.

Payroll Procedures

Once you have determined the relationship you have with your family
members is actually an employer-employee relationship, you'll have
to put payroll procedures in place. The basic payroll equation you
must follow when preparing payroll for your family business is shown
in Figure 8.1.

As you can see, Gross Pay can comprise three remuneration types:
cash, and taxable benefits, which are reported on the T4 slip, and tax-
free benefits, which are not. From this Gross Pay, the employer may take
one of two types of deductions:

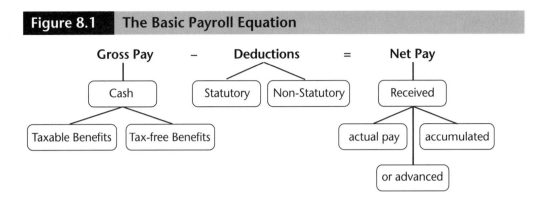

Figure 8.1 The Basic Payroll Equation

- Statutory deductions—those required by law—which are CPP, EI and Income Tax deductions
- Non-Statutory deductions, which can include deductions for union dues, registered pension plans, charities, and other deductions at the option of the workplace.

Finally, the net pay is arrived at. This can be given to the employee in cash or by cheque, deposited directly to the employee's bank account, or held or advanced.

10 STEPS IN THE PAYROLL CYCLE:

- Collect information about the employees' gross pay for the period on the Payroll Journal.
- Determine the CPP and EI premiums payable by looking up the gross earnings in the Revenue Canada Guide Books or on Revenue Canada's Tables on Diskette (TOD).
- Determine the amount of taxes to be withheld based on Revenue Canada's Form TD1 or other specialized forms filed with you by the employee.
- Calculate Net Pay on the Payroll Journal and double-check all figures.
- Calculate the Employer's Portion of CPP and EI.
- Calculate the Total Employer Revenue Canada Remittance Required for the current period for total Income Taxes Withheld, CPP premiums withheld plus Employer's Portion, EI premiums withheld plus Employer's Portion.
- Total the Revenue Canada remittance for the period. Write the cheque for the remittance.
- Prepare the bookkeeping journal entries for the payroll:

- to record the payment of the payroll
- to record the withholding amounts as a liability.
- Write the payroll cheques and double-check all to the Payroll Journal before distributing the cheques to the employees.
- Prepare a new payroll Journal for the next pay period, carrying forward all year-to-date accumulated figures.

Employer's Obligations for the CPP

Hiring an employee can be a costly undertaking for a small business. That's because the employer must make additional contributions to the Canada Pension Plan and Employment Insurance, besides the deductions that are taken for the employee's contributions.

In the case of the Canada Pension Plan, the employer must match the employee's contributions. CPP premiums do not have to be deducted from those who make less than $250 a year in agriculture, forestry, trapping, fishing, hunting, horticulture or lumbering employment, employment of a child under 18, casual employment for purposes other than normal trade or business, residence benefits of clergy, severance pay or death benefits. For a complete list check Revenue Canada's *Employer's Guide to Payroll Deductions*.

Recently, CPP premiums have taken an upward direction, as outlined in Figure 8.2.

A $3,500 basic exemption is allowed. That is, if your employee earns less than $3,500 for the year, no CPP premiums are payable. Or, in an another example, if your employee earns $6,500 in the year, and is over the

Figure 8.2	CPP Premium Rates	
Year	Rate to be paid by each Employer and Employee	Combined rate to be paid by proprietor on his/her own behalf when filing a return
1999	3.5	7.0
2000	3.9	7.8
2001	4.3	8.6
2002	4.7	9.4
2003	4.95	9.9
2004	4.95	9.9
2005	4.95	9.9
2006	4.95	9.9

age of 18, CPP premiums must be contributed on earnings of $3,000 ($6,500 – $3,500). You should also know that in the following circumstances, CPP premiums will be prorated:

1. The employee is under the age of 18
2. The employee is over the age of 70
3. The employee has started to receive a retirement or disability benefit from the CPP
4. The employee is deceased.

In the last three instances, CPP premiums are payable until the month of the event. CPP is remitted for teenagers in the month after they turn 18.

Employer's Obligations for the Employment Insurance Fund

As with the CPP, both the employer and the employee must contribute to the EI Fund. The premium payable by employers and employees will be based on an annual maximum for insurable earnings. For the years 1997 to 2000, this will be $39,000. This maximum will apply to each job the employee holds, even if this is with different employers. This means that each employer will withhold amounts for EI purposes until the $39,000 income level is reached. An employee who earns $750 a week or less will have premiums withheld all year long.

Overpayments that are made because an employee works for several employers during the year will be recoverable by filing an income tax return at year end. However, the employer gets stung here: there are no refunds for you, even if your employee has already maxed out by contributing on earnings of $39,000 or more, made with another employer. You also do not have the choice to stop contributing to the fund because the maximum was already reached for the employee with another employer.

For the year 1999, the Employment Insurance premiums will be based on a rate of 2.55% for each dollar of insurable earnings up to $39,000. That means the employee will pay maximum premiums of **$994.50,** while the employer must pay 1.4 times the required premium, for a maximum of **$1,392.30** in 1999.

Options in Making Source Deductions for Income Taxes

As an employer you should always be very careful to design compensation packages that are tax efficient for your employees. Make sure your employees complete Form TD1 *Personal Tax Credit Return,* in order for you to properly deduct taxes, according to the personal tax credits available to the taxpayer. This is particularly important when you hire teenagers who are attending university. Be sure to complete the section that outlines tuition fees and education tax credits. Never deduct more tax than necessary. Make sure you have your family members complete one of these forms each year.

Letters of Authority to Reduce Withholding

Many employers are unaware that withholding for taxes can be waived in the following instances:

- There are loss carry-overs available for claiming on this year's return.
- The following deductions will be claimed on this year's return:
  - RRSP contributions
  - Child Care Expenses
  - Moving Expenses
  - Allowable Business Investment Losses
  - Carrying Charges
  - Repayments of EI, or other social benefits erroneously paid
  - Alimony or Maintenance payments
  - Northern Residents Deductions
  - Overseas Employment Tax Credits.

The employee simply writes a letter to Revenue Canada, requesting that a Letter of Authority be forwarded to you, the employer, to waive the taxes on the amounts equivalent to the deductions above. Once you receive this Letter of Authority, file it with the employee's payroll records, and compute the payroll without taking taxes off the amounts in question.

Should you deduct RRSP contributions from your employee's salary, a Letter of Authority is not required. This is a great way to bring the benefits of a tax refund directly to the pockets of your employees, and to have their money work in the most advantageous way—tax-deferred—until withdrawal.

REAL LIFE: Tom's daughter, Tina, 16, works in her father's leather factory. He pays her $8.00 an hour, just like the other employees, to sew leatherwear on special machines. She earns $160 each week, putting in 20 hours after school and on weekends. As she is under 18, no CPP will be deducted from her pay. EI premiums would be $4.08 per week, while income tax deductions would be in the $3.00 range each week.

Tom can take 18% of Tina's earnings every week ($28.80) and contribute them directly into her RRSP; there would be no deductions for tax at all, as her income subject to tax would be only $131 per week. Assuming she would work 52 weeks in the year, Tina would earn gross wages of $8,320, but would have those set off by RRSP deductions of $1,498 for a total taxable income of $6,822, an amount below the basic personal amount ($6,456) and personal amount supplement ($500).

This family wins in several ways:

Tina gets a great start on her tax-deferred retirement savings ($1,498) as well as taking home a net pay of approximately $6,600, which she can spend or invest. (Investing of course would be the smarter option, as subsequent earnings from funds held outside the RRSP would be taxed at Tina's lower marginal tax rate.) This is $3,199 more than if her father had earned the money himself, as shown in Figure 8.3.

Figure 8.3	Splitting Income With Employed Family Members		

Tom Earns $8,320 in Profits		**Tina Works & Earns $8,320 as Employee**	
RRSP contribution:	$1,498*	RRSP contribution:	$1,498*
Taxes payable**:	$3,411	Taxes payable (EI only):	$ 212
Dollars left to family:	$3,411	Dollars left to family:	$6,610
Total dollars to family ($3,411 + $1,498): $4,909		Total dollars to family ($6,610 + $1,498): $8,108	
		Improvement:	**$3,199**

* Assumes prior-year RRSP room.
** No EI payable as owner of firm, assumes 50% tax bracket.

So, if Tom hires Tina to work in his business, income splitting will reap tax benefits. Also remember, Tom gets a tax deduction of $8,320 for Tina's gross wages, and contributes to her EI fund in the amount of 1.4 times her EI premiums ($297). This combined $8,617 deduction saves Tom $4,309 in tax dollars. So, the family is far ahead: Tina receives $8,108 in her own right. Tom saves taxes of $4,309. Revenue Canada almost strikes out, receiving only EI premiums of about $500 (employer and employee portion).

What a way to make sure it's all deductible!

Pay Tax-Free Perks to Your Family Members

A host of tax-free benefits can be paid to your family members. Here's a checklist of benefits common to small businesses for you to choose from:

Figure 8.4	Tax-Free Perks for Family

Tax-Free Benefits	Description
Wedding or Christmas Gifts that do not exceed $100; $200 in year employee marries	Not taxable, but the amount of the gift is also not deductible by the employer.
Discounts on Merchandise	This status will not extend to cases where the merchandise is purchased below the merchant's cost. A commission received by a sales employee on merchandise acquired for the employee's personal use is not taxable, nor is a commission received by a life insurance salesperson for the acquisition of his/her own policy.
Subsidized Meals	Not taxable if the employee is charged a reasonable amount that covers the cost of food, its preparation and service.
Uniforms and Special Clothing	Payments made by an employer for laundering special uniforms or for reimbursement of the employee's expenses in laundering uniforms will not be taxable to the employee.
Recreational Facilities, including memberships to social or athletic clubs	Pools, gym, exercise rooms or fees paid to be members of a social or athletic club qualify as a tax-free benefit to the employee, if it can be shown such a membership is primarily to the advantage of the employer. See IT148 and IT470.
Moving Expenses if the move was required by the employer	• Cost of movers to move and store household effects • Cost of moving the family including all travelling expenses • Cost to move personal items such as a car or trailer • Reasonable temporary living accommodations in the new work location if the new residence is not ready • Charges for alterations to furniture and fixtures that were part of the old home • Costs of cancelling a lease • Costs of discharging a mortgage • Legal fees and transfer taxes to buy a new home • Mortgage interest, property taxes, utilities and insurance to maintain the old residence after the employee has moved and the house has not yet sold, if these amounts were paid prior to February 24, 1998. • Interest costs on bridge financing if reimbursed before February 24, 1998. • Long-distance charges incurred to sell the former residence • Costs of house-hunting trips to new location • Charges and fees to disconnect telephone, TV aerials, water, etc. • Costs to connect and install utilities, appliances, and fixtures from old home • Costs of auto licences, inspections and drivers' permit fees if owned at former residence • Costs to revise wills, if necessary because of move • Certain losses on selling of home: The first $15,000 plus one-half the amount over $15,000.

Note: FMV – Fair Market Value

Figure 8.4	Tax-Free Perks for Family (Cont'd)

	Note: Such amounts paid prior to February 24, 1998, will not be taxable as long as the amount reimbursed to the employee is not more than the amount by which the cost of the home exceeds the selling price. Similarly, when an employer promises to pay an employee an amount equal to the amount by which the FMV of the home (independently appraised) exceeds the actual selling price, this will also not be taxable to the employee.
Premiums Paid under a private health services plan.	See IT339, which describes private health services plans. Also be aware that premiums paid now qualify as a tax deduction, provided certain conditions are met. The proprietor must be actively engaged in the business; self-employment income must comprise at least 50% of the individual's total income for the year or the individual's income from other sources may not exceed $10,000. As well, if the majority of employees are related to the proprietor, a maximum deduction of $1,500 for each individual and his/her spouse and $750 per child will be allowed. If non-related employees are in the majority, all premiums paid will be deductible.
Employer's Required Contribution to Provincial Health and Medical Plans	Remittances to certain Health Insurance Plans in Quebec, Manitoba, Ontario, and Newfoundland are considered to be employer levies and so are not taxable.
Attendant Costs	For the assistance of a mentally or physically challenged employee who works in your business. This provision, together with the next one, can go a long way in helping families who support employment of a disabled relative in the family business, on a tax-assisted basis.
Transportation to and from work of blind or severely impaired employees	Also includes costs of parking near the work location. A great way to help your disabled relative find a rewarding and productive work position and absorb the costs of attending the jobsite as well.
Employee Counselling Services	Not taxable if for mental or physical health or for re-employment or retirement. Therefore you can have your company pay for your relative's re-employment services once it's time for the person to move on.
Employer-Paid Training	Courses taken by the employee which enhance the employer's business activities will be received by the employee tax-free. This is a great way to have the government pay to enhance your child's resumé.
Board and Lodging at a Remote Work Site	See Form TD4 to establish tax-free status on employer-paid board and lodging and transportation at a special work site.
Subsidized School Services in remote areas	If employer provides free or subsidized school services. This tax-free benefit will not extend to a payment of an educational allowance made directly to the employee, unless the allowance covers away-from-home education of a child who is in full-time attendance at a school using one of Canada's official languages. The school must be only as far away as the nearest community to the remote worksite in which there is a suitable school.

So, as you can see, you can arrange your family's remuneration in such a way that much of it is tax-free, by maximizing opportunities to use RRSP deductions, and making a point of paying at least a portion of your family's remuneration with tax-free perks. Speak to your tax advisor about the possibilities for the coming year.

TAX ADVISOR

When hiring any employees, including relatives and family members, do the following:

Set up an employment contract This will help you determine factors of remuneration. Make sure it has the following components:

- Identifies the parties to the agreement
- Outlines the duties of the employee
- Outlines the remuneration
- Outlines vacation pay and sick leave policies
- Outlines how changes to the contract will be recorded
- Outlines non-competition agreement
- Outlines confidentiality agreement
- Outlines termination procedures
- Outlines how notices are to be given to each party
- Outlines the binding effect of the contract
- Some contracts also outline arbitration procedures.

Your legal representative may suggest other standard clauses to include in all employment contracts. It is important to put your family members on the same legal footing as others hired in your business. For this reason it is a good idea to have every employee sign a contract.

Keep Time Cards for Hourly Staff You may wish to devise a time card that looks something like the one in Figure 8.5, and then have your bookkeeper summarize the hours.

Keep Formal Payroll Records These should be summarized in a payroll register with the following components for hourly wage-earners:

- Regular Hours, Rate of Pay, Total Pay for this period and cumulative

Figure 8.5	Sample Time Card

Employee Name _____ **Emp. No.** _____

Week of _____

Day	Time		Tot Time	Time		Tot Time	Time		Tot Time	Time		Tot Time	Tot Reg hrs	Other Tot hrs	Tot Time
	In	Out		In	Out		In	Out		In	Out				
Sun															
Mon															
Tue															
Wed															
Thu															
Fri															
Sat															
Total															

- Overtime Hours, Rate of Pay, Total Pay for this period and cumulative
- CPP, EI and Tax Deductions for this period and cumulative
- Total Deductions for this period and cumulative
- Net Pay for this period and cumulative
- Cheque number.

Prepare Payroll Source Remittances These should generally be monthly, but quarterly if the source deductions owed are less than $1,000 a month. These remittances are made on a special form which will be forwarded to you regularly by Revenue Canada.

Prepare a T4 Slip One should be prepared for each family member.

Preparing the Income Tax Return Write off the gross wage expenses, and the employer's portion of CPP and EI premiums paid for employees during the year.

Sample 8.1   Claim for Salary, Wages and Benefits

Revenue Revenu
Canada Canada

STATEMENT OF BUSINESS ACTIVITIES

T2124-A
(97)

- For more information on how to complete this statement, see the income tax guide called *Business and Professional Income.*

Identification

2

Your name	Your social insurance number

For the period from:	YYYY MM DD 1998/01/01	to:	YYYY MM DD 1998/12/31	Was 1998 the final year of business? Yes ☐ No ☒

Name of business	Main product or service

Business address	Industry code (see the appendix in the *Business and Professional Income* guide)

City, town or municipality, and province	Postal code	Partnership identification number

Name and address of person or firm preparing this form	Tax shelter identification number

Business number	Your percentage of the partnership 100 %

Income

Sales, commissions, or fees		125,000 00	(a)
Minus- GST and PST or HST (if included in sales above)			
- Returns, allowances, and discounts (if included in sales above)			
Total of the above two lines			(b)
Net sales, commissions, or fees (line a minus line b)	8000	125,000 00	
Reserves deducted last year	8290		
Other income	8230		
Gross income (total of the above lines) enter on the appropriate line of your income tax return	8299	125,000 00	(c)

Calculation of cost of goods sold (enter business portion only)

Opening inventory (include raw materials, goods in process, and finished goods)	8300	
Purchases during the year (net of returns, allowances, and discounts)	8320	
Sub-contracts	8360	
Direct wage costs	8340	
Other costs	8450	
Total of the above five lines		
Minus - Closing inventory (include raw materials, goods in process, and finished goods)	8500	
Cost of goods sold	8518	(d)
Gross profit (line c minus line d)	8519	125,000 00 (e)

Expenses (enter business portion only)

Advertising	8521	5,490 00	
Bad debts	8590		
Business tax, fees, licences, dues, memberships, and subscriptions	8760	555 00	
Delivery, freight, and express	9275	1,548 00	
Fuel costs (except for motor vehicles)	9224		
Insurance	8690	1,200 00	
Interest	8710	3,560 00	
Maintenance and repairs	8960	2,468 00	
Management and administration fees	8871	9,530 00	
Meals and entertainment (allowable portion only)	8523	2,711 50	
Staff meal and entertainment expenses after Feb. 23, 1998		1,500 00	
Motor vehicle expenses	9281		
Office expenses	8810	2,879 00	
Supplies	8811	3,322 00	
Legal, accounting, and other professional fees	8860	1,526 00	
Property taxes	9180	2,478 00	
Rent	8910	12,000 00	
Salaries, wages, and benefits (including employer's contributions)	9060	35,000 00	
Travel	9200	5,890 00	
Telephone and utilities	9220	2,200 00	
Private health services plan premiums (family)		2,500 00	
Other expenses	9270		
Capital cost allowance (from Area A on page 3 of this form)	9936		
Allowance on eligible capital property	9935		
Total business expenses (total of the above three lines)	96,357 50	9368	96,357 50 (f)
Net income (loss) before adjustments (line e minus line f)		9369	28,642 50

Page 1

Courtesy of CANTAX Tax Preparation Software.

RECAP: Simple Steps to Putting Your Family to Work and Writing It Off!

1. **Pay your family members as you would a stranger.** Put them on the payroll, make sure the work is actually done, and that you pay the relative the same as you would pay a stranger for the same work.

2. **Know the difference between a sub-contractor and an employee.** Do you have a contract of service, or a contract for service? In the former case, you have an employer-employee relationship. Take stock of who has control of the relationship, who owns assets and tools, who bears the risk of financial loss for non-performance, and how the job the worker does integrates with the business itself.

3. **Know the basic payroll equation.** Gross pay, which can include cash and/or taxable benefits should be clearly defined on each employment contract and thought through with the help of a tax and a legal advisor.

4. **Put as many after-tax dollars in your employee's pockets as possible, as soon as possible.** You can do this by minimizing withholding taxes on RRSP contributions, or to adjust for child care deductions, moving expenses, or loss carry-forwards the employee may have. You can also endeavour to pay the employee as many tax-free perks as possible.

5. **Contribute the CPP and EI for your family members.** You'll be helping to create a tax-assisted pension income source in retirement, as well as a tax-assisted safety net in the ability to collect from the Employment Insurance fund, should your business fail. The tax assistance comes from the fact that the employer's portion of CPP/EI premiums is tax deductible to you. Be sure to make those contributions on time to avoid interest and penalties.

6. **Contribute to private health insurance plans for family members.** Here's a tax-free perk for the family that's deductible to the business owner, starting in 1998, provided that certain income conditions are met. There are also maximum deduction limits if your workforce comprises primarily (50% or more) of family members. See *201 Easy Ways to Reduce Your Taxes*, by Evelyn Jacks.

7. **Subsidize your employees' meals, give discounts on merchandise, pay for athletic club memberships, and employee training:** While not deductible to the business, these are great tax-free perks you can give to family members to improve their lifestyle and career paths.

8. **Make sure the young contribute to an RRSP as early as possible, with 18% of the earnings they make in your business.** This is a great way to build long-term, tax-assisted wealth quickly for your teenager.

CHAPTER 9

Often-Missed and Little-Known Family Tax Deductions

"The only true failure lies in failure to start."
HAROLD BLAKE WALKER

KEY CONCEPTS

- Tax-planning strategies exist for each member of the family to reduce taxes over the long term
- Each family member can make $6,956 in 1999 without paying one cent of tax
- Splitting of business income can result through the payment of wages to famiy members
- RRSPs for all family members with unused contribution room is desirable to tax cost average and increase Tax-Free Zones
- Investment of wages paid in your small business to family members is a great way to create the accumulation of investment earnings in that person's hands.

REAL LIFE: The Hamptons of Elm Street are a typical Canadian family. Husband Tom works as an employee for a computer consulting firm. He earns $85,000 a year plus the benefits of having a company car at his disposal. This adds a taxable amount of $5,000 to his income every year. Wife Helen stays home with her family, but has a part-time craft business she runs out of her home, grossing $25,000 annually. Daughter Suzanne, a happy 14-year-old (yes, that is a bit unusual), babysits every afternoon for the neighbours. She earns $3,500 annually. Son Cal, a 16-year-old volleyball star at his high school, has a part-time job at the local hamburger joint on weekends. His gross earnings are $7,500 annually.

There are numerous changes about to happen in the Hampton household. Tom is considering one of two career moves. He can take a management promotion within his company, and renegotiate his contract for cash and/ or benefits. Helen is on the verge of a major expansion in her business. She needs help in production and distribution, and is just about ready for a bookkeeper as well. She estimates her gross revenues next year could jump to over $50,000.

Suzanne has just received word of a remarkable opportunity. She is an up-and-coming young pianist. She has been asked to tour with a professional production company over the summertime. She would be earning $3,000 a month and living with a chaperone. Her living expenses would be covered.

Cal, showing signs of young entrepreneurship, has decided to take some extra courses after school to shore up his computer skills. He wants to get a car (doesn't every 16-year-old?) and has been looking for a few more hours at work.

This is one productive family, with all kinds of potential for tax deferral and income splitting. The problem is they don't know it, and as a result, overpay their taxes every year.

THE PROBLEM

Have you ever wondered how millionaires are created in Canada? Recent statistics tell us that currently about 1% of Canadians are millionaires and that this number is expected to triple by the year 2005. Half of our millionaires have come upon their good fortune through inheritances. Others have become wealthy through the sale of their capital assets, such as their small business corporations. Of all these millionaires, 43% have been investing their wealth in interest-producing savings; 57% have used products like mutual funds and shares. (Source: Ernst & Young Survey, *The Globe and Mail,* December 1997)

Will your family be amongst those who become millionaires in the next several years? Remember, it takes just as much time and effort to think big as it does to think small. When you think big. . .on tax savings, that is, and you will have a very good chance of joining the ranks of Canada's top earners.

THE SOLUTION

Tax planning is an activity we used to reserve for high-income earners. In the new millennium, tax planning is for everyone at every income level. Your goal is to plan tax minimization, over a period of years, as demonstrated in Chapter 2 on tax cost averaging, but to do so for each family member. If the Hamptons in our scenario above, for example, could get together, and plan their tax affairs to minimize taxes paid as a family, chances are their combined productivity would reap extra tax rewards now and in the future.

Suzanne and Cal should be as aware as their parents of current tax brackets, in order to make the most of every productive hour they work, and to know how to work their time and money around this information, now and in the future. Minimum *family* tax-planning activities should include the following:

- Maximize the use of each family member's Tax Free Zone
- Know how income diversification can increase Tax Free Zones
- Know how to split income earned by the family
- Know how to minimize "Realized Income for Tax Purposes"
- Know how to defer income
- Know how to maximize deferred investment vehicles
- Know how to find and maximize all tax credits and deductions available
- Find ways to utilize the Capital Gains Deduction within the family.

THE PARAMETERS

Following are the basic tax-planning parameters the Hamptons should apply to their family's tax plans:

Know Each Family Member's Tax-Free Zone

Tax-Free Zones are levels of income Canadian taxpayers can make without paying any taxes at all. Taxpayers and their advisors should work with the following rules, in their quest for effective income splitting within the family:

Basic Personal Amounts   Those with taxable incomes under the Basic Personal Amount plus the new Personal Amount Supplement will pay no taxes in Canada. This amounts to $6,956 in 1999 and future years, or about $580 a month.

RRSP Room   A taxpayer who earns $6,956 will build $1,252 in RRSP contribution room. So, there are two things you need to note here:

- Family members who are not taxable by virtue of the Tax-Free Zone, must still file a tax return to accumulate RRSP Contribution Room.

- Next year, the Tax-Free Zone is increased by the amount of the RRSP Room earned in the year before, provided that an RRSP contribution is in fact made. That means, the family member could make $8,208 in the Year 1999 ($6,956 + $1,252) and still pay no tax.

Other Deductions and Non-Refundable Tax Credits   Every taxpayer, including the low-income earners of the family, should strive to maximize allowable tax deductions and non-refundable tax credits, all of which will increase the Tax-Free Zone, and/or reduce net income (Line 236) to a level in which transferrable provisions can be used. More on that later.

Know How Income Diversification Can Increase Tax-Free Zone

The type of income your family members earn can also have an effect on their tax-free zone, as shown below:

Tax-Free Dividend Income Zones   Depending on where you live in Canada, the earning of dividend income can provide a substantial Tax-Free Zone. The actual amount varies from province to province, depending on whether a net income tax is in place (example, Manitoba). Let's say, that you live in Ontario, and that one spouse owns a Small Business Corporation that distributes dividends to its shareholders, which includes family members. In this case, taxpayers may earn grossed up dividends of just under $29,700, *completely tax-free*. (Actual dividends amount to $23,760 in this instance; in Manitoba a net income tax would have to be paid.)

So, if there were four family members, the family could earn about $95,000 in actual dividends, each and every year, without paying one cent of tax. This makes a strong argument for the distribution of small business profits to family members via a corporation or family trust. Speak to your tax and legal advisor about structuring such an arrangement if you own a thriving business organization.

Tax-Free Capital Gains Income Zones   To earn a taxable capital gain, the taxpayer must dispose of an asset in one of the following ways:

- Through the actual sale of the asset
- Through a "deemed disposition," which can occur:
  - When one asset is exchanged for another
  - When assets are given as gifts
  - When property is stolen, destroyed, expropriated or damaged

- When shares held by a taxpayer are converted, redeemed or cancelled
- When an option to acquire or dispose of property expires
- When a debt owned is settled or cancelled
- When property is transferred to an RRSP or other trust
- When the owner of the property emigrates
- When the owner of the property changes the asset's use from business to personal
- When the owner of the property dies.

If our taxpayer's only income of the year is from a capital gains disposition, the capital gain could be as high as **$9,275,** which translates into a taxable gain of $6,956, just under the Tax-Free Zone.

Know How to Split Income Earned by the Family

With an understanding of how to build income within Tax-Free Zones, comes another problem. How do I actually put taxable income into the hands of my family members? There are a number of ways that you can split the income earned within the family unit as a whole to accomplish the lowest overall tax cost over a period of time. To do so, though, you must be well versed in the Attribution Rules, which generally prohibit taxpayers from transferring income from the higher earner to the lower earners in order to reduce or avoid taxation. An exception to this rule is the money earned by family members who work in a family business.

For example, if Tom earned all the money in the family, $126,000 in this instance, the family tax liability would be just under $50,000. Assume, however, that $25,000 of this is earned by Helen and $7,500 by Cal. In that case, the actual family liability is approximately $35,000 — a difference of close to $15,000 in this instance. . .a year. Multiply this by Tom and Helen's approximately 40 productive working years, and you have tax savings of over $600,000, assuming no changes in earnings or tax structure.

As you can see, family income splitting is a very important life skill. In fact, when you couple income splitting with wise use of RRSP contribution room, many families could be earning part-time income completely tax-free, investment earnings on a tax-deferred basis, and paying down non-deductible debt with the resulting savings, faster. If your family is going to be working and earning money anyway, it's worth it to take a closer look at some tax-free and tax-deferred income-earning opportunities.

Stay Onside With the Attribution Rules

Money given by one spouse (the higher earner) to another (the lower earner), who then invests the sums in a non-registered account and earns interest, dividends or capital gains, will have earnings attributed back to the higher earner. In the case of minor children (those 18 or younger) gifts or transfers of money will generally be attributed back to the transferor, if the resulting investment earnings are interest or dividend bearing. However there are certain exceptions to this rule that you can use to your advantage, as outlined below.

How to Split Income Sources with Family Members   *Always document income in joint accounts and from the sale of principal residences.* The interest earnings generated from money held in a joint account will be taxed according to the ownership of the principal. That is, if the husband earned 90% of the principal, he would report 90% of the earnings. If 100% of the money in that account comes from the wife's inheritance, however, 100% of the earnings will be reported by her.

Let's say husband and wife married in their early twenties. The wife worked for a couple of years before staying home to raise a family. She contributed $5,000 to the down-payment of their first home. On the sale of that home, the family made a $25,000 tax-free gain (gains on the principal residence are tax exempt). This money was reinvested in a larger principal residence, that was later sold for a $50,000 tax-free gain. This happened two more times during this couple's marriage. Today, they have sold their last home and moved into a rented condo to maximize their travel opportunities. They have $250,000 in a joint account; the accumulated principal and gains from the tax-free appreciation of their various principal residences. In this case, subsequent investment earnings can be properly split between husband and wife, because the wife's participation in the original transaction can be traced.

Invest Tax-Exempt Sources   We earlier listed several tax-exempt income sources that, if invested by the recipient, will generate investment earnings in that person's hands. That's why it makes sense, for example, that a low-income earner who receives proceeds from a life insurance policy, an inheritance, a GST/HST Credit or tax refund, for example, should invest those sums to generate future investment earnings, which will be taxed at a low rate, if at all.

Invest in Spousal RRSPs   This is one way you can avoid the Attribution Rules now, and split income with your spouse in retirement. Give your spouse the money to invest in an RRSP. To do so, you must have actively earned income in the immediately prior year, and resulting RRSP Contribution Room. You can find out what your RRSP Contribution Room is by looking at last year's Notice of Assessment. Earnings within the Spousal RRSP will not be taxable until there is a withdrawal.

But, be careful. If the withdrawal is made within three years of the last contribution to any Spousal RRSP, the principal will be taxable to the contributor. Beyond this, withdrawals are taxed to the Spouse. A little loophole can be used when the RRSP accumulations are transferred to a RRIF (Registered Retirement Income Fund). In that case, minimum withdrawals in a Spousal Plan will not be subject to the Attribution Rules.

Grant Interest-Bearing Loans to Family Members   Spouses can loan money to each other, use the funds to generate investment earnings, and have those earnings reported for tax purposes on the return of the debtor provided that the loan bears a commercial rate of interest, and that the interest is paid at least once a year, no later than 30 days after the end of the calendar year. The higher earner must report that interest on his/her return. So don't pay the interest until January of the new year in order to defer the tax bite until April 30 of the third year.

Create Income From a Spouse's Business   If you loan your spouse the money needed to start a small business, subsequent profits and losses are taxed in the hands of your spouse. Capital dispositions, however, would be taxed in your hands.

Pay a Wage or Salary to Your Spouse or Children Who Work in Your Business   They report the income on their tax returns, you report the amounts paid as a legitimate deduction from your business income.

Transfer Dividends to Spouse   If your spouse's income is so low that s/he is not taxable, but has dividend income and the offsetting dividend tax credit, which now is going to go to waste, the higher earner can elect to transfer that dividend income and the dividend tax credit to his/her return, if a tax advantage results. The catch is that the transfer must create or increase the Spousal Amount claimable for the Spouse. The benefits, if any, will depend on the size of the transferor's income.

Invest Child Tax Benefits Received   The new Canada Child Tax Benefits and provincial Child Tax Benefits received for the child may be invested in an account held in trust for that child. If the money is untainted by birthday money or money that should be attributed to another adult, resulting interest, dividends or capital gains will be taxed in the child's hands.

Invest in an RESP for the Child   Starting in 1998, an investment in a Registered Education Savings Plan for a child under 18 will generate a new Canada Education Savings Grant from the federal government. Twenty percent of your contribution to a maximum of $400 will be granted each year. That means the maximum CESG is achieved when you put away $2,000. Earnings within the RESP accumulate tax-free, and if the child chooses to withdraw the funds later to go to a designated educational institute, the earnings and CESG grant will be taxable in his/her hands. Often that means tax-free distributions to the student. Speak to your tax and financial advisor about the nuances of this new plan and make a contribution at the end of every year to maximize savings opportunities with the CESG.

Invest in a Child's RRSP   You can gift your child money to invest in his/her own RRSP. Resulting investment earnings will be tax-sheltered until the child withdraws the money from the plan. However, the child must have "earned income" which creates RRSP Contribution Room. To register this with Revenue Canada, the child must have actively earned income sources, and file a tax return to report them every year.

Invest Gifts From Grandparents Who Live Offshore   The Attribution Rules can be avoided on money received from non-resident grandparents or other relatives, provided the money is held in trust for the child and not used by adults for any other reason.

Accumulate Tax-Free and Tax-Deferred Income Within Life Insurance Policies   Usually it costs little to invest in a child's life insurance policy, and this can grow to a lucrative tax-free estate in some cases. Speak to your insurance advisor about this.

Know the Taxation of Income and Assets on Death of a Spouse   While the Attribution Rules can create hurdles for you during your lifetime, at death, Revenue Canada does show a bit of consideration. That is, most assets can be transferred to your spouse on a tax-free basis. This includes accumulations within an RRSP, RRIF, other annuities, as well as the transfer of assets held outside a registered plan. In the latter case, the assets may be transferred to the spouse at the adjusted cost base calculated for the deceased, or at Fair Market Value (which means the capital gain, if any, is reported on the final return of the deceased, if this is advantageous), or at any amount in between.

Transfers of assets to children are usually at fair market value in death as in life, with the exception of certain farming assets, and transfers of RRSP/RRIFs to dependent children in cases where there is no surviving spouse. But you should receive tax advice before filing the final returns of a deceased taxpayer and, better still, in anticipation of your tax status, well before death. For example, life insurance policy proceeds are received by beneficiaries on a completely tax-free basis. The time to arrange to pay for such a policy. . .is when you are healthy. Look into it now.

Know How to Minimize "Realized Income for Tax Purposes"

Another basic taxation concept you should keep in mind as you plan your family's financial affairs now and into the future is how much tax you'll pay on the next dollar of income that's earned. This is important, as the next dollar could push you or your family members into a new tax bracket, which will take a larger tax bite. Using a knowledge of marginal tax rates and what you know of the tax benefits of income splitting and diversification, you'll be able to make tax-wise decisions on future investments together with your advisor. This can be as important as asset allocation within an investment portfolio.

For example, if your income exceeds $59,180, you live in BC, and you earn your next dollars as dividends, you'll give up about 36% of your dividend earnings to the taxman. However, had you earned this extra income as salary, interest or pensions, you'd lose about 53% of this to taxation. Get the picture? The return on your investment in astute tax planning is about 17%. . .a number too large to ignore.

So, the trick is to plan your affairs to generate only a certain level of "realized income" for tax purposes each year. Here are some suggestions.

• Split income sources receivable over two tax years: i.e., severance, bonuses, RRSP withdrawal, sale of capital assets. (Example: dispose of one-half of duplex owned in each of two tax years.)
• Offset capital gains generated in the year with prior year capital losses.

- Create future wealth by investing in capital assets: increasing values are never taxed until disposition of the asset. Then plan dispositions strategically around capital loss availability, and income inclusion over a period of years.
- Optimize opportunities to reduce tax rates with special tax provisions applied to dividends, certain foreign pensions (U.S. Social Security; German Pensions), scholarship and bursary income, and small business corporations/qualifying farm properties.
- Utilize tax-exempt income planning opportunities (i.e., estate planning with life insurance policy proceeds; tax-free retirement pension income creation through investments in universal life insurance policies, RESP enhancements through the Canada Education Savings Grant, etc.).
- Always look closely at your "income mix" for tax purposes.

Example: The taxpayer has capital accumulations outside an RRSP of $1,000,000. He is expecting a rate of return of 12.5% on average from his investments. Approximate tax liabilities will be:

Figure 9.1	Taxes on Invested Capital of $1 million	
Income Source	**Average Tax Payable**	**Effective Tax Rate***
All interest, salary, pensions	$51,553	41%
All dividends	$30,591	25%
All capital gains	$35,425	28%

* ETR takes into account the progressive tax structure that gives preferences to income up to $29,590 and income over $59,180, as previously discussed. The figures above represent average annual taxes payable. (Taxpayers will want to work out actual federal/provincial results in individual provinces.)

In short, by realizing a minimum amount of "taxable income" every year with investment diversification, tax sheltering and income splitting, average Canadians can significantly reduce their tax burdens over time.

Know How to Defer Income

Two factors should be considered here: (1) lack of indexation and (2) declining tax rates for some.

Our tax brackets and other key figures are not indexed upward unless the inflation rate exceeds the Consumer Price Index by more than 3%. Since 1992 we've had no indexing adjustment, which means that average Canadians are paying tax at higher rates, sooner.

Assuming that income earned up to $29,590 is taxed at a combined federal/provincial rate of 26%. Had this tax bracket been indexed, let's say by 2% per year since 1992, it would today stand at over $33,000. In addition, had indexing of 2% per year been used to adjust personal amounts, our Tax-Free Zone would have been over $7,200 by now; more than the 1999 Basic Personal Amount and Supplement. So Canadians pay taxes with inflation-eroded dollars. Yet, with the introduction of the Personal Amount Supplement and the reduction to the Federal Individual Surtax starting in 1998, it looks like taxes will be coming down for some. Low- and middle-income taxpayers who had deferred income out of the 1997/1998 tax year were wise: income today will be taxed more advantageously.

Therefore, if tax rates drop consistently over the next few years, a dollar invested in a tax-deferred savings plan today will bring higher after-tax rewards. Also, by deferring investment income to the future, when tax rates and/or your income may be lower, you will keep more.

Maximizing Tax-Deferred Savings
- Shelter as much of your taxable income as possible with RRSPs, RESPs, RRIFs; and tax-exempt life insurance policies are another useful vehicle.
- Take any unsheltered portion of your upcoming severance package over two tax years, if possible.
- Acquire appreciating assets, holding them outside your RRSP. Those appreciating tax-deferred assets will build real dollar value for the future. In the meantime, use the information in this chapter to plan your realized taxable income and offsetting deductions and tax credits wisely.
- If you are comfortable with borrowing money to invest in assets held outside your registered accounts, do so after tax analysis, writing off interest expenses today in return for wealth accumulation tomorrow. It is worthwhile discussing such investments with your tax advisor.

Look at every tax dollar saved today as a bonus paid to you and your family.

Ordering of Investments

There is a certain order in which you should arrange your tax affairs to minimize non-deductible expenditures and maximize deductions and credits. This should be discussed with your financial planner, and may include the following:

Letter of Authority   If you or any member of your family earns employment income, be sure to write to Revenue Canada and request that a Letter of Authority be forwarded to the employer to make RRSP contributions directly to your RRSPs and not to deduct taxes from the amounts transferred.

Pay Off Non-Deductible Debt   Credit card balances attract obscene interest rates. Pay those off first. A smart way to do this is to make an RRSP contribution, reap your tax savings and then pay off your credit cards.

Turn Non-Deductible Debt Into Deductible Debt   Borrow for investments placed in non-registered accounts; the interest for these will be deductible, while the interest paid on money borrowed to invest in RRSP/RESP accounts will not be. Opening a home-based business and claiming home office expenses will make your interest costs partially deductible; or you can borrow against the equity in the home, place investments in non-registered accounts and then write off the interest on the loan.

Maximize RRSP Room   The first way to do this is to file a tax return each and every year in which you have "earned income." This includes the following sources earned by each taxpayer:

• Salary or wages before the deduction of Employment Insurance, Canada Pension Plan or RPP contributions, employee contributions to a retirement compensation arrangement or the cleric's residence deduction.

PLUS:

• Income from royalties from a work or invention of which the taxpayer was the author or inventor (Line 104 of the return)
• Net research grants (Line 104 return)
• Supplemental unemployment insurance benefits (Line 104)
• Employee profit-sharing plan allocations (Line 104)
• Net rental income (Line 126)

- Alimony or maintenance payments or repayments included in income, including support payments received by a common-law spouse (Line 128 of the return)
- Net income from carrying on a business where the taxpayer is actively engaged in the daily operations, either alone or as a partner (Lines 135 to 143)
- After 1990, income received from a CPP/QPP Disability Benefit (Line 152)

LESS:

- Refunds of salary, wages or research grants
- Union dues or professional dues paid (Line 212)
- Other employment expenses (Line 229)
- Current-year losses from carrying on an active business (Lines 135 to 143)
- Current-year net rental losses (Line 126)
- Alimony or maintenance payments deducted or repaid (Line 220)
- Any amount included in business income that represents the excess negative balance from dispositions of eligible capital property over and above recaptured deductions previously taken.

Once earned income is known, the figure is multiplied by 18%. The result is then compared to the maximum dollar limits for the tax year. The lesser of the two is used in the calculation of the RRSP deduction claimable on Line 208.

Note: To maximize your annual RRSP contribution in the years 1996-2003, you must have earned income of $75,000.

Shelter RRIF Income   Once you are ready to take a taxable pension from your RRSPs, you should decide what income level you will want to create with your withdrawals, being mindful of Tax-Free Zones for the lower-earning spouse, and tax bracket levels for the higher earner. It is generally best to withdraw the money from a sheltered plan in the hands of the lower earner first, to bring income up to either the Tax-Free Zones, if the person has no other income, or the income falls within the upper limit of the first tax bracket ($29,590 or less).

Or, Generate Tax on Sheltered Earnings Now   These planning strategies work for those under age 70, the year in which you must report your first withdrawals under the RRIF (Conversions from RRSP to RRIF must be made before the end of the year in which the taxpayer turns 69). However, if the taxpayer will be in a higher-income bracket after retirement than before, or because of a spouse's death, it may make sense to generate some tax at the current lower level of income, rather than wait for it all to be taxed at the highest marginal rates.

Maximize Sheltered Education Savings   Put your Canada Child Tax Benefits into an RESP to generate the Canada Education Savings Grant from the federal government. Up to $2,000 per year may be contributed; the government will then generate a grant of up to 20% or $400. Better still, hold your CTB monies outside a registered fund placed in trust in the child's hands, because resulting investment income will be taxed to the child. Then also make the RESP investment, if you can afford to do both.

Maximize Investments in Life Insurance Policies   If you have already paid down non-deductible debt, maximized your RRSP contributions and your children's education savings, consider investing in a life insurance policy with an investment component to maximize tax-sheltered proceeds for estate planning purposes. Most universal life plans also feature the option to withdraw portions of the policy on a tax-free basis.

Know How to Find and Maximize All Tax Deductions and Credits Available

You probably are noticing a trend: a tax saving in the hand today is worth two in the bush tomorrow. There are two types of tax reducers available, and you should know the value of each:

* tax deductions
* tax credits.

Tax Deductions   There are three types of deductions to look out for as well. The first are deductions that reduce your gross income sources, to arrive at Total Income on Line 150. The second grouping is deductions that reduce Total Income on Line 150, used in determining net income on Line 236. The third grouping reduces Net Income to arrive at Taxable Income on Line 260. This is the figure upon which federal taxes will be calculated.

The value of a tax deduction is directly proportionate to your marginal tax rate. If your marginal tax rate on income is 31%, each tax deduction you can find will reap a return of 31 cents on the dollar. If your marginal tax rate is 51%, each deduction is worth 51 cents on the dollar as well. So, the higher your income, the greater the value of a tax deduction, until you reach taxable income of $59,180. Every dollar in tax deductions after this point will reap the same value: the equivalent of the top marginal tax rate.

For taxpayers in income ranges between $19, 456 and $53,215, a range of "clawback provisions" exist, which can actually increase your marginal tax rates even more. It is therefore most important that you find every tax deduction available to you if you qualify for the following tax provisions on your return:

CLAWBACK ZONES FOR CANADIAN TAXPAYERS

- Old Age Security (payments are clawed back when individual net income exceeds $53,215)
- Employment Insurance (payments are clawed back when individual net income exceeds either $39,000 or $48,750, depending on the type of benefits received and number of weeks since June 1996 the taxpayer collected EI benefits)
- Child Tax Benefits (clawbacks begin when *family net income levels* reach $20,921)
- GST/HST Credits (clawbacks begin when *family net income levels* reach $25,921)
- Age Credits for those who reached age 65 in the year (clawbacks of the credit begin when the individual's net income exceeds $25,921)
- Personal amount supplements: amounts are clawed back after net income exceeds $6,956.

When we speak of refundable tax credits like the Child Tax Benefit or the GST/HST credits, every extra dollar of Net Income on Line 236 will shave off monthly income for needy families. It pays to do your "tax homework" in those cases particularly. Reducing your Net Income on Line 236 is key to both tax savings and tax-free income to lower-income earners.

Here are some items that will help:

Figure 9.2	Deductions that Reduce Gross Income to Arrive at Total Income on Line 150	

Income Source	Deductions Allowed	Documentation Required
Employment Income on Line 101, net of any Clerics Housing Allowance, which is reported instead on Line 104	Certain specified out-of-pocket expenses, including board and lodging expenses of truck drivers, auto, travel, home office and sometimes promotion and entertainment expenses of commissioned salespeople.	Must be supported by a signed Form T2200 from the employer; all receipts and log books must be available in case of audit.
Clerics Housing Allowance on Line 104	The amount of the housing allowance, generally noted on the T4 Slip is deducted on Line 232 of the return.	None other than a properly completed T4 Slip.
Net Research Grants on Line 104	The cost of out-of-pocket expenses incurred in the research process.	A statement itemizing list of expenses.
Wage Loss Replacement Benefits	The cost of premiums paid by the employee since 1968 can offset this income.	Obtain a statement from your employer to verify this amount.
Foreign Pension Income	A deduction is allowed on Line 256 for certain pension income amounts, based on tax treaties.	An accounting of the income received, and the foreign exchange rate must be available.
Rental Income	Operating expenses of running the revenue property, including capital cost allowance. Some restrictions apply.	Records of all income receipts, operating expenses, auto logs, and capital acquisitions and dispositions, mortgage fees and payments, etc.
Taxable Capital Gains	Costs of outlays and expenses including brokerage fees and appraisal fees.	All income reports from brokerage houses, and sale of other properties including cost of improvements; expense receipts.
Other Income	The first $500 of income from scholarships, fellowships, bursaries is tax-exempt; also the first $10,000 of death benefits received from a deceased's employer recognizing the deceased's contributions or unused sick benefits. In the case of retiring allowances, rollovers into an RRSP qualify for an RRSP deduction on Line 208; sometimes a deduction for legal fees is allowed on Line 232 if the taxpayer had to fight to establish rights to the severance.	Keep all supporting documentation for any income sources reported here, including payments for serving on a jury, RESP distributions, payments out of a retirement compensation arrangement, interest earned on loans made for investment purposes to lower-earning family members, annuity payments not reported as pension income.

Figure 9.2	Deductions that Reduce Gross Income to Arrive at Total Income on Line 150 (Cont'd)

Income Source	Deductions Allowed	Documentation Required
Self-Employment Income from unincorporated small businesses, professional practices, commission sales agents, farmers or fishermen.	All reasonable operating expenses incurred to earn income from a business with a reasonable expectation of profit, including a deduction for Capital Cost Allowance on business assets.	All supporting income deposit records, receipts and logs for all business expenditures and asset acquisitions and dispositions.

Deductions That Reduce Total Income on Line 150 to Arrive at Net Income (Line 236)

- Registered Pension Plan deductions from Box 20 of T4 slips or Box 32 of T4As
- Registered Retirement Savings Plan deductions
- Union, Professional or like dues
- Child care expenses, as computed on Form T778
- Attendant care expenses
- Business investment losses, as computed on a statement attached to the return
- Moving expenses, as computed on Form T1M
- Taxable Child/Spousal support payments
- Carrying charges on your investments, like interest and safety-deposit box fees
- Exploration and development expenses
- Other employment expenses, as computed on Form T777 or TL2, including artist's and musician's expenses
- Other deductions on Line 232, including legal fees incurred to collect salary and wages owed to the employee, establish a right to a retiring allowance, enforce payment of maintenance amounts previously established as payable, to appeal an assessment of tax, interest or penalties under the Income Tax Act, Employment Insurance or Canada Pension Plan
- Clawback calculation of Employment Insurance or Old Age Security.

Deductions that Reduce Net Income to Arrive at Taxable Income on Line 260

- Employee home relocation loan deduction as itemized on your T4 Slips
- Stock option and shares deduction as itemized on your T4 slips

- Other payments deduction for social assistance, worker's compensation or federal supplements reported on Lines 144 to 146
- Limited partnership losses of other years
- Non-capital losses of other years
- Net capital losses of other years
- Capital gains deductions
- Northern residents deductions
- Additional deductions for vows of perpetual poverty, net employment income from the United Nations and its agencies, income exempt under tax treaty, alimony or child support received from a U.S. resident.

The deductions discussed above will be itemized in detail under the Tax Advisor section of this chapter. Make sure you flag anything that could apply to you or your family members.

Tax Credits

There are two types of tax credits:

Refundable ones like the Canada Child Tax Benefit, the Goods and Services Tax Credit, and a host of provincial refundable tax credits. Both spouses must file a tax return to receive these amounts, as the credits are dependent on your net family income. Those age 19 and over should also file to recoup their own Goods and Services Tax Credit.

Non-Refundable Tax Credits, on the other hand, are the allowances the government makes for personal circumstances that warrant consideration under the tax system. These amounts are found on page 3 of the T1 General Return, and provide the same benefit to all taxpayers, regardless of income level. That is, the total allowable amounts allocated to each credit is totalled, multiplied by 17% to arrive at the Total Non-Refundable Tax Credits to be used to reduce federal taxes payable on Schedule 1 of the return. Because provincial tax credits are based on the level of federal taxes — after non-refundable taxes — one must consider the combined federal/provincial benefit in assessing the value of missed non-refundable tax credits.

Following are the real dollar values you'll obtain every time you make an effort to maximize your personal tax credits, like medical expenses, charitable donations and tuition/education transfers from your university-bound children. Don't miss out on tax-reducing personal tax credits. Check out their most-current dollar values with your tax advisor.

Figure 9.3	Value of Additional Personal Tax Credits for taxpayer in the top marginal rates*

BC	AB	SK	MB	ON	PQ	NB	NS	PE	NF	YK	NWT
31.75	26.94	31.27	31.03	29.48	38.62	29.56	29.11	29.49	31.26	27.29	26.01

* Source: Tax Facts and Figures 1998, PriceWaterhouseCoopers.

To put these numbers into a real life context, consider the example of a disabled taxpayer, Joe Smith, 79, who has been blind since 1988. A widower, he has failed to obtain a Form T2201 *Disability Tax Credit Certificate* and missed out on his Disability Tax Credit for 10 years. This credit is listed on the return as $4,233. In real dollar terms, the credit is worth 31.75% of $4,233, as Joe lives in BC. That amounts to $1,344 a year! In filing an adjustment to claim his Disability Tax Credit all the way back to 1988, Joe tapped into a jackpot. . .Revenue Canada sent him back over $13,000. *A five-figure return in tax savings!*

THE TAX ADVISOR

Having understood the basic parameters of family tax planning, and the claiming of tax deductions and credits, you will now want to know and implement the following strategic plans with your professional advisors:

Tax Planning Strategies for Minors
- Save income attributed to the child (like Child Tax Benefits) in a separate bank account, untouched by gifts or other transferred funds from adult relatives.
- Invest a child's employment or self-employment earnings; then have the higher-income earner in the family pay for consumer goods. Resulting investment income is either not taxed at all (if under the Tax-Free Zones) or taxed at low rates.
- Make sure the minor files a tax return. Actively earned income sources, from part-time jobs, including work in the family firm, qualify for the building of RRSP room.
- Gifts may be made to a minor child; however, resulting earnings in the form of dividends or interest are taxed back to the adult, until the child turns 18. The only exception to this rule is the earning of capital gains, which can accumulate in the hands of the child.
- Contribute to an RESP for your minor children, in order to take advantage of the Canada Education Saving Grant and tax-deferred accumulations of earnings.

Tax Planning Strategies for Net Incomes under $25,921

- Utilize all tax deductions to reduce net income, including full RRSP room, to avoid clawbacks of refundable tax credits, and Personal Amount Supplement .
- Separated couples may wish to revisit old taxable support payment agreements in light of generous new federal/provincial Child Tax Benefits (CTB), particularly if recipient and payer are both in the lowest tax brackets. Enhanced Child Tax Benefits could bring more tax relief than the support payments deduction.
- Optimize the Surtax Reduction for 1999. One way to do this is to consider earning more taxable dividends in your investment portfolio and by maximizing non-refundable tax credits like medical expenses and charitable donations.
- Maximize newly enhanced Child Care Expense claims (up to $7,000 for children under the age of 7 and $4,000 for those age 7 to 16. Special provisions available for disabled children and students).

Tax Planning Strategies for Net Incomes of $25,921 to $75,000

- These income ranges are in the "Clawback Zones": where marginal tax rates can increase dramatically as social benefits are clawed back through the tax system. This includes the value of The Age Credit, Canada Child Tax Credits (CCTB), GST Credits, OAS receipts, EI Benefit.
- Maximize RRSP contributions, and any other tax deductions on Lines 207-234 of the tax return.
- Income diversification and income-splitting opportunities are vital in this income range. Find ways to legitimately transfer income to lower earners in the family.

Tax Planning Strategies for Net Income over $75,000

- Always make your maximum RRSP contribution
- Plan to average realized taxable income in business and investment portfolios and add Labour Sponsored Tax Credits to the mix
- Implement plans to give to charity, political parties, to maximize tax savings opportunties over a period of years
- Transfer medical expense credits to lower earners in the family
- Make sure any transferable credits (Age Amount, Pension Income Amount, Tuition & Education Credits and Disability Credits) are properly claimed and that lower earner's income levels are properly computed to maximize these claims.

Tax Planning for Taxpayer's Death

- As a regular part of their tax and financial planning activities, individuals should prepare a tax projection every year to anticipate tax liabilities should unexpected death occur, particularly if there are valuation changes in the non-registered investment portfolio.
- Life insurance policy requirements should be closely reviewed, to cover potential tax liabilities and for the purposes of leaving a tax-free estate to the family.
- RRSP/RRIF beneficiary elections should be made and wills updated to ensure hassle-free rollover of assets to the proper beneficiaries.
- Remember, RRSP/RRIF accumulations of the second surviving spouse are fully subject to tax upon that person's demise. This generally means the estate will lose 50% of its accumulations to tax. Perhaps that survivor, who may be at a lower tax bracket in life, should consider generating the tax on the registered funds by withdrawing and reinvesting funds in a non-registered account, or possibly a universal life insurance policy.
- Bring forward unused capital/non-capital loss balances for use on the final return.
- Discuss planned giving for those whose estates are adequate and already cover family concerns.

Preparation of Specific Tax Plans

- The family should prepare an RRSP savings plan for each member.
- The family should prepare an education savings plan, with participation from parents, children and grandparents, if possible.
- Those who are employed in the family should prepare a tax calculation to determine the value of cash and benefits from their employers, to better prepare for future employment negotiations.

ACTION PLAN: DOCUMENT OFTEN-MISSED AND LITTLE KNOWN FAMILY TAX DEDUCTIONS

Take a moment now to work through our family tax write-off checklist in Figure 9.4.

Have you forgotten any of the following common tax write-offs? If so, tap into Revenue Canada's Fairness Provisions. That is, you can apply to recover missed tax deductions and credits, all the way back to 1985, provided you forward a letter (or Form T1ADJ) outlining the error or omission and attaching receipts.

Figure 9.4   Check List of Tax Savers*

Tax Deductions

- ❑ RRSP Contributions for each family member
- ❑ Union or professional dues paid
- ❑ Child Care Expenses paid
- ❑ Attendant Care Expenses of the disabled
- ❑ Business Investment Losses
- ❑ Moving Expenses
- ❑ Taxable Spousal Support
- ❑ Taxable Child Support (agreements before May 1, 1997, or certain specific purpose or third party payments)
- ❑ Repayments of Employment Insurance
- ❑ Repayments of Old Age Security
- ❑ Repayments of Worker's Compensation
- ❑ Payments of Legal Fees for objecting to an assessment or appeal under the Income Tax, EI, CPP or QPP legislation, collection of late child support payments, collection or establishment of a right to retiring allowances or pension benefits
- ❑ Repayments of scholarships, fellowships, bursaries, research grants, retiring allowances or Canada Pension Plan benefits
- ❑ Repayments of refund interest paid by Revenue Canada
- ❑ Refunds of undeducted RRSP contributions made after 1990 and received in the tax year.

Tax Credits

Non-Refundable Federal Credits

- ❑ Claim for Basic Personal Amount
- ❑ Claim for Personal Amount Supplement
- ❑ Claim for Spousal Amount
- ❑ Claim for Equivalent-to-Spouse Amount
- ❑ Claim for Infirm Dependant over 18
- ❑ Claim for the Age Credit (65 & older)
- ❑ Claim for the Caregiver Amount
- ❑ Claim for the Disability Amount (be sure to obtain a Form T2201 signed by the attending medical practitioner)
- ❑ Claim for the $1,000 Pension Income Amount
- ❑ Claim for Tuition/Education Amount
- ❑ Claim for Student Loan Interest Amount
- ❑ Claim for Transfers from Spouse, including the Age, Disability, Pension Income and Tuition/Education Amounts, depending on how many of these amounts are available, and the spouse's net income
- ❑ Claim for Medical Expenses, the excess of total expenses for the best 12-month period ending in the tax year, over 3% of net income, to a maximum limitation of $1,614
- ❑ Claim for Donations and Gifts, usually based on a limit of 75% of net income; this two-tiered credit can be calculated with unclaimed donations of the prior five years. Group family claims together to exceed $200 a year to maximize tax savings.

Refundable Tax Credits

- ❑ The Child Tax Benefit
- ❑ The Goods and Services Tax Credit
- ❑ Provincial Child Tax Benefits
- ❑ Overpayments of Canada Pension Plan Premiums
- ❑ Overpayments of Employment Insurance Premiums
- ❑ The Refundable Medical Expense Supplement
- ❑ Refunds of investment tax credits
- ❑ Employee and partner GST/HST rebates
- ❑ Overpaid tax installments
- ❑ Provincial/Territorial tax credits

* Attach supporting documentation

Now, check off the specific tax deductions allowed to investors and the self-employed:

Figure 9.5	Write-Off Tax Deductions of Investors

Tax Deductions

❑ Line 127: Capital gains income is reduced by outlays and expenses like:
- brokerage fees or legal fees
- appraisal fees or surveyors fees
- finders fees or commissions
- advertising costs
- transfer taxes

❑ Line 126: Revenue Property Owners may write off operating expenses like:
- mortgage interest, insurance, property tax
- maintenance and repairs
- accounting fees, advertising, office stationary costs, travelling expenses in certain cases, utility costs, condo fees
- management fees, landscaping fees. When claiming Capital Cost Allowances on assets, you may not create or increase a loss with this deduction

❑ Line 221: Carrying Charges. Interest and dividend income can be offset by claiming interest expenses, safety deposit box fees, accounting fees, investment counsel and management fees for assets held outside an RRSP/RRIF/RESP.

Tax Credits

❑ Line 301: The Age Amount, claimable by those who attain age 65 during the year, but reduced if net income exceeds $25,921.

❑ Line 314: The Pension Income Amount, claimable by those who received a periodic pension from superannuation, or those aged 65 or older who receive private periodic pension income sources. Those who receive these amounts as a result of the spouse's death will also qualify.

Figure 9.6	Write-Off Tax Deductions of the Self-employed

Tax Deductions

- ❑ Accounting Fees, Legal Fees
- ❑ Advertising, Marketing and Promotion
- ❑ Asset Repairs and Maintenance
- ❑ Assistant's or Other Employee's Salaries
- ❑ Auto Expenses
- ❑ Bad Debts
- ❑ Board and Lodging while on the road
- ❑ Bonding and Licensing
- ❑ Business Meals and Entertainment (50%)
- ❑ Capital Cost Allowances on Assets
- ❑ Car Washes
- ❑ Commissions paid to Sub-contractors
- ❑ Convention Expenses (2 per year)
- ❑ Disability-Related Expenses
- ❑ Fines and Penalties if normal risk of earning income
- ❑ Gifts to clients and employees (may give one tax-free gift per year to each employee of up to $100; $200 in year of marriage; but these amounts are not deductible by employer)
- ❑ Insurance and Interest costs
- ❑ Leasing costs for building or equipment
- ❑ Office-in-the-Home expenses
- ❑ Telephone and other Communications Costs
- ❑ Other operating expenses

Tax Credits

- ❑ Canada Pension Plan contributions payable on Self-Employment income
- ❑ Investment Tax Credits on specified asset purchases
- ❑ Taxes paid during the Year by Instalment.

RECAP: A Dozen Ways To Make Sure It's Deductible!

The purpose of this chapter was to empower you to expand your tax cost averaging activities to the returns of the entire family. You can do this by:

- finding ways to maximize Tax-Free Zones
- diversify income sources
- transfer income, deductions and credits from one family member to the other
- minimize realized income in the year
- defer income to the future
- maximize deferred investment vehicles and
- maximize the tax deductions and tax credits available to you.

You can also:

Tax cost averaging for all family returns. Remember to:

- Apply carry-forward provisions to each return this year, if available and appropriate.
- Transfer as much income as possible to lower-income earners, according to the Attribution Rules.
- Have higher earners spend on consumer goods, lower earners save and invest their earnings.

Order Tax Affairs Properly:

- Minimize Withholding Taxes from Employment with a Letter of Authority
- Pay off non-deductible debt
- Turn non-deductible debt into deductible debt
- Maximize RRSP contributions for each family member
- Plan to shelter future RRIF Income
- Plan to shelter education savings
- Plan to enhance your tax-free estate with life insurance benefits
- Create new money with proper use of tax deductions/credits
- Minimize exposure to clawbacks on family tax returns.

Create Family Equity with Your Small Business

This topic is discussed in more detail in our next chapter.

···

CHAPTER 10

How to Create Serious Wealth

"Only you can hold yourself back, only you can stand in your own way. . .Only you can help yourself."
MIKHAIL STRABO

KEY CONCEPTS

- Every business owner should discuss with advisors the format of the business's organization every year
- Incorporation offers specific tax advantages for income diversification
- Qualifying businesses could receive tax-free capital gains of up to $500,000 on the sale of shares (or a qualifying farm property)
- Family ownership of qualified shares can enlarge tax-free gains
- Thinking ahead and thinking big can reap tax rewards.

REAL LIFE: When Thomas started his software development company out of his basement office a couple of years ago, he would have never guessed what paths his business venture would take him on.

Those first years were so lean. Thomas barely scratched together enough money to lease his computer. But he had an idea, and a dream. This, together with his determination to create, led to the building of a base of institutional buyers of his custom-designed software. His income rose steadily. From a loss of $10,000 in the first year, to a profit of $60,000 in Year 2, $120,000 in Year 3 and before looking into Year 4, Thomas realized he was paying altogether too much tax.

Thankfully, it was at this point that he made some strategic tax-planning moves that really paid off. You see, quite out of nowhere, Thomas would be approached to sell his business.

THE PROBLEM

How can there possibly be a problem? Not only did you survive the start-up years, but you are bringing home more money than you ever did working for someone else. It gets even better: next year you'll bring home more, and as time goes on, you can see the dramatic growth in your business venture.

The problem, is that many start-up entrepreneurs fail to anticipate just how quickly their business can take off. This is particularly true of those who start their businesses because of otherwise negative circumstances — the loss of a job for example.

What's important is to understand that every business enterprise has the potential to earn profits, and in the background, to build equity. The technology, product, distribution method and client base is the value that some other firm may wish to acquire some day. This is an opportunity that has significant tax consequences, and if set up properly, the structure of the venture can bring hundreds of thousands of dollars more into your family's coffers.

THE SOLUTION

Every business owner should be discussing the format of the business organization with his or her tax advisor every year. Should you be incorporated or should you keep your proprietorship?

The answer is often one of timing. For example, you may wish to earn start-up losses in a proprietorship, in order to offset other income of the year — perhaps from a severance package. Or, if there are excess losses, you may wish to carry them back and offset employment income earned in the best of the last three tax years.

You will also want to be conscious of your RRSP contribution opportunities. Net business income of $75,000 will reap maximum contribution room of $13,500.

However, when it comes to *selling* your business, incorporating your proprietorship has several advantages:

- The opportunity to design a compensation package for shareholders, who are also employees, that may encompass employment income, as well as the distribution of dividends from the company's after-tax profits
- The opportunity to earn tax-free capital gains through the use of the $500,000 Capital Gains Exemption.

In Thomas's case, the opportunity to sell his business came in Year 3. He was offered $2 million for his little software company. Due to his effective tax planning, Thomas's family kept much of that money for themselves.

THE PARAMETERS

The $500,000 Capital Gains Exemption is available to taxpayers who own shares in a qualifying small business corporation, or a qualifying farm property. Specific rules of eligibility must be met, however, before the claim for the deduction can be made.

A Qualified Farm Property

For those taxpayers who disposed of qualified farm property during the year, the available Capital Gains Deduction (CGD) must be reduced by any Capital Gains Deduction previously claimed. If you are unsure of this information, contact Revenue Canada for a record of previously used amounts. Then the least of the following will determine the deductible amounts:

- annual gains limit from dispositions of qualified farm property during the current year
- the available CGD, and
- the cumulative gains limit.

The definition of "qualified farm property" that was acquired after June 17, 1987, includes real property owned by the taxpayer, spouse or child for at least 24 months immediately before sale.

Also, a gross revenue test must be met; that is, in at least two years prior to disposition, gross income earned by the individual by active farming operations, must exceed net income from all other sources.

Third, all or substantially all of the fair value of the farm assets must be used in active business operations for at least 24 months prior to disposition.

Different rules exist for farms acquired before June 17, 1987. The $500,000 Capital Gains Exemptions will be allowed, but only if the farmland and buildings were used in an active farming business in Canada in the year of sale, and in at least five years prior to the disposition.

For 1988 and subsequent tax years, eligible capital property (for example, farm quotas) will constitute qualified farm property eligible for the deduction if used in the course of carrying on the business of farming in Canada.

Shares of Small Business Corporations

The $500,000 Capital Gains Exemption for individuals has been available on the disposition of qualified small business corporation shares after June 17, 1987. The allowable deduction is calculated as the least of the following four amounts:

- For 1988 and 1989, $333,333 (66 2/3% × $500,000) less any amount claimed as a capital gains deduction in prior years (adjusted for increased inclusion rates). After 1989, the available deduction will be $375,000 (75% of $500,000) less any amount claimed as a capital gains deduction in prior years (adjusted for increased inclusion rates)
- The individual's cumulative gains limit less any amount deducted as a capital gains deduction in respect of qualified farm property for the year
- The individual's annual gains limit less any amount deducted as a capital gains deduction in respect of qualified farm property for the year
- Net taxable capital gains for the year from dispositions of qualified small business corporation shares after June 17, 1987.

What is a qualified small business corporation share? The share must be a share of the capital stock of a small business corporation owned by the individual, his/her spouse, or a partnership of which s/he was a member.

A small business corporation is defined to be a Canadian-controlled private corporation in which all or substantially all of the assets (90% or more) are used in an active business or carried on primarily in Canada by the corporation.

The share must not have been owned by any person or partnership other than the individual or a person or partnership related to him/her throughout the 24 months immediately preceding the disposition. During the holding period, more than 50% of the fair market value of the corporation's assets must have been used in an active business.

Finally, if the taxpayer disposes of shares of a small business corporation, some of which do not meet the holding requirement, the shares are deemed to be disposed of in the order in which they were acquired.

TAX ADVISOR

When setting up a qualifying small business corporation, it is important to give thought to the ownership of the shares, asset transfer provisions and compensation packages. The initiative is complicated and requires significant planning. However, Figures 10.1 and 10.2 serve to make an important point: the use of the $500,000 Capital Gains Exemption can help qualifying small business owners accumulate serious wealth.

In the case of Thomas's sale, had he been the sole shareholder of his corporation, his tax liability would have been calculated as follows, assuming no prior use of the CGD:

Figure 10.1	Sole Shareholder Uses CGD
Tax Provision	**Calculation**
Proceeds of Disposition	$2,000,000
Adjusted Cost Base	$ 1
Capital Gain	$1,999,999
Taxable Gain (3/4)	$1,499,999
Less Capital Gains Deduction (3/4 × $500,000)	$ 375,000
Net Taxable Gain	$1,124,999
Taxes Payable @ 50%*	$ 562,500

* Consult with advisors for accurate calculation for your province of residence.

Now, let's assume that Thomas and his wife Pat each were shareholders of this Small Business Corporation. Now, each could split the gain and use their Capital Gains Exemptions, if available:

Figure 10.2	Capital Gains Split With Two Shareholders	
Tax Provision	**Thomas**	**Pat**
Proceeds of Disposition	$1,000,000	$1,000,000
Adjusted Cost Base	$ 1	$ 1
Capital Gain	$ 999,999	$ 999,999
Taxable Gain (3/4)	$ 749,999	$ 749,999
Less Capital Gains Deduction (3/4 × $500,000)	$ 375,000	$ 375,000
Net Taxable Gain	$ 374,999	$ 374,999
Taxes Payable @ 50%*	$ 187,500	$ 187,500

* Consult with advisors for accurate calculation for your province of residence.

The family pockets $187,500 more in tax savings. Imagine how much more of the $2 million they could keep if each of their adult children had also owned shares in this SBC. Therefore, it pays to set up your business in anticipation of future windfalls. Ask your advisor about minimum tax and net income tax implications.

The transfer of assets from a proprietorship to a corporation, the timing of such an event and the structure of the shareholders' agreements and compensation structures all need careful consideration. These matters should therefore be discussed with your tax advisor.

RECAP: Half a Dozen Ways to Accumulate Serious Wealth

1. **Structure the timing** of the creation of a Small Business Corporation to maximize tax advantages the proprietorship may have (i.e., excess loss carry-overs).

2. **Structure your salary** within a Small Business Corporation at least to maximize annual RRSP contribution room.

3. **Consider distributing shares** of the company to your spouse and adult family members in order to multiply the claims for the $500,000 Capital Gains Exemption.

4. **Try to envision the value of your business enterprise** after Year 1, Year 3 and Year 5 and determine valuation method and reporting requirements with your advisors.

5. **Anticipate the changes that rapid growth** will mean to the financial management of the company. Also consider what structural changes the growth of your business will require in the short term, including financing for expansion.

6. **Creation of a Family Trust** is something you should discuss with your advisor.

Remember, Think Big. . .it takes as much effort as thinking small, and it's much more fun!

CHAPTER 11

How to Turn a Tax Audit into a Profitable Experience

"To know is to control."
SCOTT REED

KEY CONCEPTS

- Under Section 18(1) (a) and (h) Revenue Canada may question whether an outlay was made to incur income from a business or property, and whether the expenses were really personal or living expenses of the taxpayer
- Under Section 152(7), Revenue Canada has the power not to accept your tax return as filed and may make its own assessment of the amount of tax it believes you should pay
- Section 152(8) makes the assumption that Revenue Canada is correct in its assessments, unless those assessments are challenged by the taxpayer
- Therefore, the Burden of Proof is on the taxpayer to disprove Revenue Canada's assessment
- The taxpayer and his advisor should be aware of tax law and its changes over a period of years in order to determine the best final outcome for the audit.

REAL LIFE: Rubin was staring down his tax auditor's nose. "I have every receipt for every number I claimed on my tax return, every deposit of income. There should be absolutely no problem with any of the numbers on the tax returns you are checking so thoroughly. " It was hard to hide the disdain from his voice. Three years earlier, Rubin had been through a similar tax audit, just as he was turning the corner on the popular acceptance of his passionate compositions.

   After years of working at the Symphony as an employed classical guitarist, and writing music in between performances, Rubin got his first major break. A popular singer from Vancouver, heard his piece, *Majestic Moonlight*. Despite incurring nothing but losses for his efforts over the previous three-year audit period, that chance meeting opened doors to a recording contract. The royalties from Rubin's first CD were just starting to flow, when Revenue Canada reassessed Rubin's previously filed tax returns, and disallowed his business losses. Citing no reasonable expectation of profit from what they considered to be his "hobby" of songwriting, Rubin faced a tax bill of $18,000, due to the disallowed business losses that he had used to reduce his other income.

At the time, Rubin fought a hard battle with Revenue Canada. Together with his tax advisor, he successfully proved there was a reasonable expectation of profit, forfeiting only his auto expense claim, because he had failed to keep an auto log. Not long after this, Rubin got his first royalty cheque: $55,000—more than what he earned at his day job in a year! Then the new opportunities started to roll: an offer to become Composer in Residence for the Toronto Symphony Orchestra, concert dates, radio interviews. . .Rubin had survived his first tax audit and was on his way to fame!

Which brought him back to the present. Three months ago, he was visited again by Revenue Canada. In the excitement of the developments in his career, he had failed to file tax returns over the past two years. When he did comply, after several reminders, Revenue Canada decided to scrutinize his figures closely. Rubin had been concerned about the visits from the auditor, who observed his recording studio, located in his newly renovated home. Three weeks before Christmas, Rubin learned that he had become the subject of a *net worth assessment,* when a reassessment proposal indicated he faced another potentially devastating, retroactive tax bill.

THE PROBLEM

Sometimes, a taxpayer can get the feeling s/he's between a rock and a hard place. While struggling to make a business run in the early years, the biggest threat s/he faces in a Revenue Canada tax audit, assuming documentation requirements are met, is the possibility that an auditor will disallow legitimate business losses by using the "no reasonable expectation of profit" argument. The onus of proof, however, is on the taxpayer to show there was a reasonable expectation of profit at the time the expenditures, and the effort, occurred.

Then, wouldn't you know it, a few years later, having made a success of the struggle to succeed, the taxpayer faces a completely different problem, but similar subjectivity: the danger of being accused of under-reporting income, due to a subjective assessment of living standards, under the Net Worth Assessment process. The onus of proof that income was not under-reported? Again, it's on the taxpayer.

As a result, many taxpayers shiver with dread, when they anticipate the receipt of a tax audit notice. The potential for a subjective dismissal of their documented claims is often enough reason to underclaim expenses. For this reason, many taxpayers give up their rights under the law and deliberately overpay their taxes. . .year in and year out.

While the law grants the privilege of self-assessment on the self-employed, "grey areas" in the law can create uncertainty and unfairness. The taxpayer should be able to have the peace of mind and the confidence that comes with knowing the tax return was filed to his or her best benefit under the framework of the law, and is audit-proof.

THE SOLUTION

In complying with tax law, the self-employed person automatically accepts the Burden of Proof that income reported is correct and that deductions were allowable, reasonable, incurred to earn income from a venture with a reasonable expectation of profit, and backed up with documentation.

That Burden of Proof is actually your best weapon against a subjective judgement from Revenue Canada. It presents an opportunity for you to explain your business motives, and therefore to exercise your full legal rights under the Income Tax Act. Because nobody knows your business and its potential in the future as well as you do, you have a distinct advantage going into a tax audit. You have the opportunity to control the outcome.

When you combine the expert knowledge you have of your business vision for today and tomorrow, with excellent tax expertise of your financial advisors, the result should be audit-proof tax returns that reduce your overall tax costs over the period of years in which you run your business. It is critical, though, that the audit strategy both you and your advisors will employ is decided upon *at the time your tax returns are being filed*. This is the key to winning a tax audit.

THE PARAMETERS

In assessing your tax-filing game plan throughout the year and during tax-filing season, there are three things to analyze and discuss with your tax advisors:

Your Audit Risks

Anticipate these facts: a civil servant, your tax auditor, has both the opportunity and the power to second-guess your business acumen, without the assistance of objective rules to follow in assessing whether your business is viable or not, or to test whether you are indeed reporting all of your income. The auditor's interpretation of how you conducted your business activities can initiate a long and costly dispute that could be left to the courts to rule who is right. You can avoid this with proper documentation of the facts.

Your Audit Tests

When your taxes are in dispute there are five tests you must pass:

- that the activities of the business result in a source of income
- that there is a reasonable expectation of profit from the venture over time
- that deductions claimed are reasonable under the circumstances, and supported by receipts
- that all income from the venture is being reported
- that all personal use components of any expenditures are removed.

We have discussed most of these concepts in previous chapters.

Your Tax Audit Strategy

To go into an audit battle with a winning strategy, arm your defense team with a number of deft weapons:

- the story of the evolution of your business: yesterday, today and tomorrow
- full use of your appeal rights
- research of precedents set in similar cases by the courts
- a summary of the tax law of the day, current tax law and future tax proposals
- an Action Plan that includes your Tax Audit Strategy.

The Evolution of Your Business   We have suggested earlier, that your Daily Business Journal will go a long way in helping to inform your tax auditor about the motive and intent you have in operating your business. So will the log of networking activities, business plans, budgets, cash flow projections, marketing plans and human resource plans you pull together with your bookkeeper, as previously discussed.

Don't wait for a tax audit to put these documents in place. File them with your tax return each and every year, *in anticipation of an audit*. Be prepared.

Rights to Appeal   There are a number of important rights you should be aware of and discuss with your tax advisor. Here are just a few of them:

Right to Voluntary Compliance   If you have indeed overstated your business deductions or under-reported your income, you need not fear any penalties for gross negligence or tax evasion, if you contact Revenue Canada first and ask that your tax return be corrected. There may be some interest charges, and Revenue Canada will expect you to either pay any resulting bill or make satisfactory arrangements to pay it over time. There may also be a late-filing penalty if you failed to file on time. However, the best policy is to correct and amend those tax returns to comply with the law, as soon as possible, even if you have to do this in retrospect. However, be sure to speak to your tax advisor about these matters before contacting Revenue Canada.

Right to a Fairness Committee Review   If you have suffered an unusual hardship beyond your control—illness, natural disasters, death of a family member and so on—and as a result of this were unable to file a tax return, interest and penalty costs can be waived through a decision of Revenue Canada's Fairness Committee. (See *The Complete Canadian Home Business Guide to Taxes* by Evelyn Jacks for a sample letter and detailed criteria for making such a claim.)

Right to Object to the Assessment or Reassessment   Discuss with your advisors the appeal routes available to you should you run into a dispute with Revenue Canada.

Consequences of Non-Compliance   Throughout this book we have assumed the reader is a law-abiding citizen who endeavours to file a correct tax return to his family's best tax advantage, as allowed under the law. Following are consequences of failure to comply with tax law, for those who want to know the parameters:

Figure 11.1	**Summary of a Tax Payer's Appeal Rights**

Method of Appeal	**Basic Parameters**
1. Informal Objection	When you perceive a mistake has been made in the initial assessment of your return, have your tax advisor write to Revenue Canada to request an adjustment. If Revenue Canada refuses to make the adjustment, and you still believe they are incorrect, contact your tax professional immediately to discuss further options.
2. Notice of Objection	This is a formal objection to the Chief of Appeals at the local Tax Services Office. It must be filed within one year after the taxpayer's filing due date or 90 days after the day of the mailing of the Notice of Assessment, whichever is later. You may indicate in this Notice that you wish to appeal directly to the Tax Court of Canada.
3. Appeals to the Tax Court of Canada	An appeal may be made after the Minister has confirmed the assessment or reassessed, or within 90 days after the service of a Notice of Objections to which no reply has been received. This court has an informal procedure, for federal taxes in dispute of $12,000 or less, and a general procedure for amounts over this, which requires the services of a lawyer. This court may dispose of the appeal by either dismissing it or allowing it in whole or part.
4. Appeals to Federal Court of Appeal	If you have lost an appeal at the Tax Court level, informal procedures, you have 30 days from the date the decision was mailed to you or your representative to appeal to the Federal Court. A lost case under the general procedure may be appealed to the Federal Court within 30 days from the date on which the judge signs the decision. The months of July and August are omitted; so if the decision date was June 30, the taxpayer would have until September 30 to file the appeal.
5. Appeals to the Supreme Court of Canada	Appeals to the Supreme Court require the granting of permission to hear the appeal by the Supreme Court itself. The taxpayer has 60 days from the date of the judgement at the Federal Court of Appeal to file an application. The month of August is left out.

Figure 11.2	**Consequences of Non-Compliance**

Circumstance	**Penalty**
Failure to file a return on time	5% of unpaid taxes plus 1% per month up to a maximum of 12 months from filing due date, which is June 15 for unincorporated small businesses
Subsequent failure to file on time within a 3-year period	10% of unpaid taxes plus 2% per month to a maximum of 20 months from filing due date
Failure to provide information on a required form	$100 for each failure
Failure to provide Social Insurance Number	$100 for each failure unless the card is applied for within 15 days of the request

Figure 11.2	Consequences of Non-Compliance (Cont'd)

Circumstance	Penalty
Failure to provide information with regard to foreign-held property	$500 per month for a maximum of 24 months; $1,000 a month for a maximum of 24 months if there is a failure to respond to a demand to file plus an additional penalty of 5% of the value of the property transferred or loan to a foreign trust or the cost of the foreign property where failure to file exceeds 24 months
Gross negligence: false statement or omission of information in the return	50% of tax on understated income with a minimum $100 penalty
False statements or omissions with regard to foreign properties	5% of the value of the property, minimum of $24,000
Late or insufficient instalments	50% of interest payable exceeding $1,000 or 25% of interest payable if no instalments were made, whichever is greater.
Tax Evasion	50% to 200% of tax sought to be evaded and imprisonment for up to 5 years
Failure to deduct or remit source deductions	10% of amount not withheld, or remitted
Second such failure in same year	20% of amount not withheld or remitted if this was done knowingly or through gross negligence.

Research Precedents on Tax Law

It can really pay to ask your tax advisors how taxpayers in similar businesses to yours have argued their cases in the courts. Probably one of the most contested concepts in Canadian income tax law is Revenue Canada's enthusiasm for charging "no reasonable expectation of profit" as the condition for disallowing the losses of small business owners. As this continues to be problematic for small business owners, it is useful to see what conclusions the judges of the Canadian court system have come up with over the years.

John R. Owen of Thorsteinssons, Toronto, tackled the issue of the assessment of "reasonable expectation of profit" and produced an excellent summary of cases in the *Canadian Tax Journal (1996) Vol. 44, No.4.* Some of the more important cases, and their conclusions are summarized on the following pages.

REAL LIFE: National Trust Co. Ltd. (R.R. McLaughlin)

This case concluded, amongst other things, that whether a business can be considered to have a reasonable expectation of profit depends on the taxpayer's *motive and conduct*, and not necessarily the result of his or her efforts. The taxpayer was found to have a going concern with a reasonable expectation of profit, even though the venture did not in fact break even in almost 30 years.

The concept? When attempting to justify losses incurred in your business, be prepared to show that your motives and conduct were to build a business with a reasonable expectation of profit. Keep a detailed Daily Business Journal, as described in Chapter 4.

REAL LIFE: Moldowan

Mr. Justice Dickson made several comments about reasonable expectation of profit that have been quoted in subsequent cases. The judge concluded that in order to have a taxable "source of income," it follows that there must be a profit or a reasonable expectation of profit. Whether there is a reasonable expectation of profit "is an objective determination to be made from all the facts. . .and the following should be considered":

- Profit and loss experience in past years
- Taxpayer's training and background for the business being run
- Taxpayer's intended course of action for the future
- The capability of the venture as capitalized to show a profit, after charging capital cost allowances
- The acknowledgement that these factors will differ with the nature and extent of the undertaking.

The concept? What we have here is five clues to winning a tax audit. Be sure you write a synopsis of the events and characteristics of the business and its owner to answer the issues above. Revisit the issues annually and file your presentation with your tax files.

REAL LIFE: Tonn

In this case, the presiding judge took yet another view of the issue, stating the following: "The tax system has every interest in investigating the bona fides of a taxpayer's dealings in certain situations, but it should not discourage, or penalize, honest but erroneous business decisions.

The tax system does not tax on the basis of a taxpayer's business acumen, with deductions extended to the wise and withheld from the foolish. Rather the Act taxes on the basis of *the economic situation of the taxpayer. . .*for most cases where the department desires to challenge the reasonableness of a taxpayer's transactions, they need simply refer to section 67. This section provides that an expense may be deducted only to the extent that it is reasonable in the circumstances."

The Court went on to say this about the previously mentioned Moldowan case: "The primary use of Moldowan as an objective test, therefore, is the prevention of inappropriate reductions in tax; it is not intended as a vehicle for the wholesale judicial second-guessing of business judgments."

The concept? You must be prepared to show that the expenditures you made in the business were reasonable in relation to income earned and projections for future growth, in order to properly assess your economic standing for tax purposes at the end of the tax year. Also be prepared to provide background information about the reason for business decisions, and why you made the judgement calls you did, to justify that you run an ongoing concern.

REAL LIFE: Urquhart

In this case the judge asked the following question: "Is hard work and time spent enough to warrant the deductibility of losses?" The taxpayer in this case did not show actual profitability from the venture he was running and failed to show potential profitability in the foreseeable future. Therefore, no reasonable expectation of profit was present and losses were disallowed.

The concept? Taxpayers and their advisors must make an honest assessment of ventures that are on continual shaky ground financially. Why would you continue to pour personal resources into a venture that amounts to nothing but a deep money pit? At what point do you see a return on your investment of time and money? Is there something you need to communicate about the expectation of profit? Does a contract exist? Is it imminent? Or should you concede that what you have is indeed a hobby, or even a passion, but not a business that will ever turn a profit? In that case, reduce income earned to nil only. This can be the right decision in certain circumstances.

REAL LIFE: Johns-Manville Canada Inc.

This case commented on a basic concept in tax law: "that where the taxing statute is not explicit, reasonable uncertainty or factual ambiguity resulting from lack of explicitness in the statute should be resolved in the favour of the taxpayer."

The concept? The conclusions of this case are very important to every taxpayer who fears subjectivity in a Revenue Canada audit. The courts should rule with leniency and give you the benefit of the doubt, if you are otherwise a model tax-filing citizen attempting to comply with tax laws that lack certainty and objectivity.

This overview of some of the interesting comments of learned judges on the "grey area" of the reasonable expectation of profit test, provides some insight into the difficulty the courts face in dealing with subjectivity resulting from the Income Tax Act. You might glean the following guidance from these outcomes:

- Your motive and conduct will influence reasonable expectation of profit
- Profits and losses, as well as your qualifications to run the business and your investment in income-producing assets will help to establish the probability of future taxable income sources
- Strive to properly present your economic situation in real terms, but as they relate to the evolution of your business over a period of years. Make sure your return is assessed with tax cost averaging in mind
- Revenue Canada should not penalize taxpayers who try to make an honest self-assessment of their liabilities within the framework of the law.

Know the Tax Law of Yesterday, Today and Tomorrow

One of the interesting aspects about going through a tax audit is the fact that the auditor is usually focused only on assessing the tax years in question. This is generally the current year and/or two years back. He or she is not necessarily concerned with the concept of "tax cost averaging." This is where you and your advisor come in. Make sure the auditor prepares your reassessed return with all the most advantageous tax provisions allowed by the law of the day and subsequent tax law.

It is also important to note that, while adjustments to CCA claims must generally be made within 90 days after receipt of Notice of Re/ Assessment, a tax auditor will generally allow adjustments to the CCA statements during a tax audit. If a tax bill results, for example, you may wish to pull out all the stops and claim full CCA for the year. You'll also want to claim as many carry-over provisions as possible and review claims with family members, especially if there are transferable provisions available.

You and your tax advisor must see to it that the end result of a tax audit reflects tax-planning provisions that are available.

For an overview of recent business tax changes, see Chapter 12.

Also remember that while the Burden of Proof is on the taxpayer to disprove Revenue Canada's reassessment of taxes, it is Revenue Canada that must prove any additional facts that are raised during the audit, or in tax evasion cases, that there was wilful intent on the part of the taxpayer to defraud the government. The taxpayer may also challenge the appropriateness of Revenue Canada's penalties under the circumstances and to request that these be removed if they are excessive or incorrect.

Remember, *Section 152(8) makes the assumption that Revenue Canada is correct in its assessments, unless those assessments are challenged by the taxpayer.* Therefore it is most important that the taxpayer make a pro-active effort to prove the tax return was correct as filed. This position is important, and should set the tone throughout the audit process.

TAX ADVISOR

The taxpayer and his advisors should follow certain steps pro-actively in ensuring the taxpayer's rights under the law are upheld during a tax audit. Initiate your Tax Audit Strategy in two parts:

A. Initial Audit Assessment Steps

1. Act immediately. Go to see your tax advisor, with all the records you can find for the tax years being audited.
2. Determine key dates to be met: the deadline for filing a Notice of Objection, for example, is the first milestone. Determine whether this document should be filed, and when.
3. Have your advisor request an extension from Revenue Canada, in order to pull together the documents required. This will take some of the pressure off, and allow you to continue with your normal income-producing activities while you put together the tax audit case. But from here on in, do not miss any agreed upon dates or tasks in your dealing with Revenue Canada.
4. Identify the problem areas in your position, like missing receipts or logbooks, as well as the subjective issues: no reasonable expectation of profit or the accuracy of the auditor's net worth assessment.
5. Identify the problem areas in Revenue Canada's position, including misinterpretation of the actual facts, errors in assumptions made, omissions of facts in making the assumptions, and so on.

6. Anticipate your outcomes: Quantify your upside and your down-side. Your upside would be one of two things:
   - No changes are made to the return
   - You uncover a tax-filing method, or new receipts that have been previously missed, and use these to actually have your taxes de-creased for the year.

   Your downside could be one of three things:
   - Taxes are increased because source documents are missing
   - Taxes are increased because tax losses are disallowed
   - Taxes are increased because income reported is adjusted upward.

   Put numbers to these circumstances to analyze your financial risk factor.

7. Identify the tax provisions that were new for that year, to ensure you took advantage of them all, and understand their carry-over poten-tial. Keep a list of these in your tax files. See page 186 for a list of the Top 10 Questions you should ask your tax advisor.

8. Determine and agree upon your Tax Audit Action Plan.

9. Set aside the time to work with your tax advisor in putting together the appeal.

10. Be prepared to go back and look through old files, recover duplicate receipts, create auto logs from the information in your Daily Busi-ness Journal, etc. A tax audit will require your personal resources of time and money.

B. Tax Audit Action Plan

1. File the Notice of Objection once all the documentation has been gathered.

2. Organize your evidence: the documents that support your tax re-turn as filed, any other additional documents, a listing of all relevant facts in your case to support your filing position, and a listing of facts that will reply to Revenue Canada's assumptions. It would be a good idea for all of these facts and replies to be organized in such a manner that they can be referred to quickly and often. A tabular numbering system, set out at the start of the process, generally saves everyone a lot of time.

3. A taxpayer is within his/her rights to ask Revenue Canada to dis-close the facts behind all of their findings, and the exact provision in the law that supports these facts.

4. It is important to stick to the facts at all times. You and your tax advisor must separate emotion from fact to win the case. Embellishment that is not supported by fact can sink your case, and, besides, is probably unnecessary anyhow. Remember, you have more facts than Revenue Canada does, because you know the truth: what actions were taken in the past and why, and what potential there is for the business for the future. Judges understand that you did not have the benefit of hindsight when you acted as you did.

5. Neither you nor your advisors should express personal opinions within your written materials or at the audit interview (see below). Word your positions to say "Our position is the following." This keeps your presentation at a high level of professionalism.

6. Correspond with Revenue Canada in writing throughout the audit. For example, ask Revenue Canada to put any requests for additional information in writing.

7. Identify your weaknesses at the outset. If you don't have an auto log, say so. Often, the auditor will allow the taxpayer to go back and look through any documentation that will show a business driving pattern, and submit a summary of this. Another strategy that sometimes will work, is to start keeping an auto log immediately, even if this is throughout the audit period. A long shot, it will at least give the auditor a trend to look at.

8. Identify any tax provisions you may have missed in that tax year, or prior years. This is a good idea at any time, as you always want to be in a position to recover missed provisions. You can of course, open prior-filed returns all the way back to 1985 for most provisions. In fact, it may pay to find a reason to do this to assist in your audit position. For example, if you missed claiming your safety deposit box fees, prepare an adjustment to your prior-filed returns to claim these. Now you have 90 days from the date on the Notice of Reassessment to open up claims for Capital Cost Allowances elsewhere on the return. This could reduce your net income, CPP liability, tax liability, perhaps even create or increase your spouse's claims for the Spousal Amount, and so on.

If it's a downside you are facing, you'll need to pull some rabbits out of a hat to pay the bills; reviewing prior-filed returns for errors or omissions is a good way to find new money.

During the Audit Interview

Generally, once all the information is gathered, the taxpayer's advisor will meet with the auditor to impart the information and have a discussion about the file. It is not generally a good idea for the taxpayer to participate in this process. You should let your hired advisor do the communicating at this point. Consider the following:

1. Meet with your advisor once more before the interview with the auditor and overview the materials and the strategy once more. This is a good rehearsal for your advisor, who may have some last-minute questions. What you are hoping for at this point is that you have communicated the story of your business, your intent for its future, and why the tax return should be accepted as originally filed. Because you will have all of these facts in writing, you should have peace of mind and confidence in your advisor to represent you with all the details you feel are important to express to the auditor.

2. The advisor should begin the presentation of the materials with a solid overview of the essence of the taxpayer's position, and what information is enclosed to support this position. It is important that this information is assembled so that the auditor can review it easily.

3. Once the facts of the position and the supporting documents are identified, the advisor should proceed to explain how these items relate to the way the tax return was actually filed. It is at this time that new provisions to be included should be identified, or prior errors on returns should be corrected.

4. The advisor has the opportunity to gather additional information needed by the auditor to come to his/her conclusions about the file. Therefore, if the advisor doesn't know the answer to the question, or the auditor needs additional information, this should be written down, and confirmed with the auditor — in writing — as the pieces of information required to satisfy the process.

5. The advisor then should clearly articulate the conclusion the taxpayer wishes to see, including the details of specific provisions (additions or deletions) and how they should be filed. With regard to subjective conclusions, the advisor should be prepared to stand firm on the reasons why the return was filed the way it was, and in the case of tax losses why the taxpayer is within his right to believe his assumption of reasonable expectation of profit from the venture. The advisor may cite previous cases that address the theory of the law, present information about changes in the tax law that apply to the taxpayer, as well as the documents that support the future growth of the business.

6. Remember that the case of *Johns-Manville Canada Inc.* established that where there is reasonable doubt, the case should be resolved in

favour of the taxpayer. This is especially true if the law is ambiguous or uncertain. In the end, the judge of a dispute must look to the Income Tax Act for guidance in coming to a decision. If it can be shown that the taxpayer attempted to comply with the law as it stands (without the benefit of hindsight at the time his/her actions were taken) and that the law does support the taxpayer's position, Revenue Canada's subjective interpretation of the Act is the weaker position.

Examples of Cases in Which Taxpayers Profited From the Audit Experience

While the following are based on true stories, all characters and circumstances have been changed for anonymity, and any similarities to actual circumstances are purely coincidental.

REAL LIFE: Taxpayer A had succeeded in receiving a patent for an invention

After attempting on numerous occasions to manufacture the invention through a third party — only to find one manufacture was about to go bankrupt, another failed to perform after numerous delays in the schedule — the taxpayer proceeded to manufacture the invention on his own. He invested the money required to redraw plans, bought the required materials and set out to build the prototype, and in the process claimed all the expenses on his tax return. This created an operating loss which offset the income from the inventor's day job — working as a letter carrier. Revenue Canada disallowed those losses citing no reasonable expectation of profit.

In contesting this reassessment, the taxpayer was able to show, despite sketchy records, the motives and intent in attempting to find a manufacturer for the invention, and that the invention would already have been in the marketplace, had it not been for the aborted manufacturing attempts with the first two companies. In fact, the taxpayer had detailed cash flows and projections to show how close he was to bringing the invention to market. He was about to close a contract to sell 50 of his inventions to a national distributor on a consignment basis. In fact, in the time since he filed the tax returns in question, a number of steps had been taken to enhance the expectation of profit. All of these events since the taxes were filed formed part of his audit strategy.

At the end of the process, the auditor agreed that there was indeed a reasonable expectation of profit from the business, and the taxpayer's returns were reassessed, only this time more advantageously than when he first filed. That's because his sharp tax advisor had caught a little-known provision about writing off the costs of a patent. Rather than using a straight-line method over the life of the patent, which is the usual course of actions, a fast write-off, introduced in 1993, allowed the taxpayer to claim the costs over a 4- to 5-year period instead of a 17-year period. After this adjustment was made, Revenue Canada actually owed the taxpayer money!

REAL LIFE: Taxpayer B had a farming enterprise

It ran losses for years, as he faced one calamity after another. From bad weather to insects to bottomed-out world market pricing, this taxpayer fought to stay afloat. In fact, he came close to losing his asset on several occasions. While he was under this economic siege, he failed to file tax returns. A badly disorganized bookkeeper, Taxpayer B simply ignored Revenue Canada's requests to file a return until one day he was faced with a Net Worth Assessment.

This is a little-known audit tool Revenue Canada employs from time-to-time under the powers given to it under Section 152 (7) of the Act. This process begins like any other tax audit: income verification as well as receipts are requested. Then, the tax auditor sits back and takes a close look at the taxpayer's perceived surroundings and lifestyle. What they saw in Taxpayer B's circumstances was vast landholdings, Christmas vacations financed by his wife's earnings as a government worker, and a paid off-mortgage. . . which in truth, was the result of a family inheritance.

Taxpayer B was a classic case for a net worth assessment. He owned tax-paid holdings, but had little evidence of income to justify the apparent wealth. Further, he failed to give an explanation when questioned about it. The auditor took a stab at assessing the value of his lifestyle, guessing at what he thought income might have been in the audit period, to pay for it all. Given the powers in the Act, the auditor computed income, deductions and credits accordingly, and sent out a bill for tens of thousands of dollars. Taxpayer B was literally in tears.

The good news, is that at the end of a very lengthy challenge to disprove the net worth assessment, which included combing through crates of disorganized receipts, bank records, contracts and asset transactions, Revenue Canada owed Taxpayer B over $15,000. To his great relief, even after paying his tax deductible accounting fees, Taxpayer B's net worth actually took a jump, when the audit process was finished.

Has he been a regular tax filer since? You guessed it. . .no! Some people are just their own worst enemies!

RECAP: A Half a Dozen Ways to Profit From a Tax Audit

Like it or not, the fact that you are in business for yourself increases your chance of a tax audit. One way to deal with this fact is to continually prepare yourself for a potential audit, together with your tax advisor as you file your income tax returns annually. Remember these rules:

1. **Know your rights under the law.** The four basic provisions in the Income Tax Act which give the self-employed taxpayer guidance in self-assessment of their tax burden are the following:

   - A taxpayer's income for a taxation year from a business or property is the taxpayer's *profit* from that business or property (Section 9(1))
   - No deduction for an outlay or expense will be allowed unless it was made for the purpose of gaining or producing income from a business or property that has *a reasonable expectation of profit*. These deductions must not include personal living expenses (Section 18)
   - No deduction for an outlay or expenses will be allowed except to the extent that it was *reasonable* under the circumstances (Section 67)
   - Whether you filed a return or not, Revenue Canada may reassess the taxes payable arbitrarily because they are *not bound to accept a return* as filed by the taxpayer. (Section 152 (7)).

2. **Never cave.** It is critical to be pro-active when you're audited. Know that under Section 152(8), Revenue Canada's assessment of your taxes will be accepted as fact, unless you exercise your burden of proof and challenge Revenue Canada's assumptions.

3. **Make it a point to be a model Tax-Filing Citizen.** File a tax return every year, on time, to minimize penalties and build up points for when you really need them. . .at tax audit time. Disorganization is absolutely no excuse. Be sure to hire help if you can't — or don't want to — keep your own records in order. Besides, for small business owners it's deductible!

4. **Make sure it's all deductible**. . .defend your right to claim losses in the current year and the carry-over years by emphasizing the source of income created by your activities and that by their very presence you meet the test of "reasonable expectation of profit."

5. **Gain confidence from the facts.** A judge must give the taxpayer the benefits of reasonableness, if you are making an effort to comply with the Income Tax Act. Your Burden of Proof puts you in a position of power to win a tax audit. . .provided that you stick to the facts, and remain highly professional in your approach. In many cases, Revenue Canada owes money to the tax filer at the end of the audit session.

6. **Never give Revenue Canada to question your integrity.** The Income Tax Act allows you tremendous leeway to reduce gross income with legitimate tax deductions and credits that will average out your tax burden over time. Tax fraud is just not worth it. Make sure you support all income sources—cash, cheque, credit card, barter—with paper documentation and separate bank accounts. Keep receipts for all personal non-taxable sources, like inheritances, so that you can prove that what you have is fully tax paid. When it comes to your tax compliance burden, honesty is the best—and cheapest—policy over the long term.

7. **Know why we audit taxpayers.** The answer is quite simple: to promote a level playing field for all business owners in Canada. To illustrate, we'll leave you with this story:

   Karl is in the construction business. He bases his quotes and his profit margins on the fact that he'll be paying GST and income taxes every year. His competitor, Shady Sal, on the other hand, quotes "under the table." That is, he'll cut the price in half to get the job, and he figures he can do this, because he's paying no GST and no income taxes. Can Karl compete? The answer is apparent.

   The integrity of the tax system depends on Revenue Canada to crack down on characters like Shady Sal, and to protect honest taxpayers like Karl. Auditing tax returns of the self-employed is a part of this process.

CHAPTER 12

Taxpayers and Their Advisors: The Top Check Lists

"Don't forget until too late that the business of life is not business, but living."
B.C. FORBES

KEY CONCEPTS

- Choose your tax advisor with care; this can be the most profitable long-term relationship you have with an advisor
- Start your relationship with your advisor by reviewing prior-filed returns, all the way back to 1985, to make sure you haven't forgotten to claim an expenditure that's tax deductible
- Communicate your financial planning goals, as well as your business objectives to your advisor. Make sure the advisor has a keen understanding of where you want to be in five years
- Ask your advisor to help you keep current on tax changes specific to small business owners for both current and prior years. This knowledge can be helpful in a tax audit in the future
- Spend more time with your tax and other financial advisors throughout the year to help you make tax-oriented planning decisions for your current affairs and for your estate.

REAL LIFE: Marshall, a self-employed plumber, was getting married. . .and he had a deep, dark secret that he didn't want his bride to know about. In fact he was so worried about this, he found himself waking up frequently in the middle of the night, in a complete sweat. Now, his wedding date was fast approaching, and he had to confess to somebody. . .Marshall hadn't filed a tax return. . .ever.

You cannot imagine the relief on poor Marshall's face, after he found out that the statute of limitations required that he only file for the current year and two years back. He had done the right thing, the last time he woke up in a sweat: he called a local tax accountant with a very good reputation and an understanding demeanour. He explained that he just didn't want to go into his new marriage with this terrible burden hanging over him.

A week later, when his returns were filed, he just couldn't believe that Revenue Canada actually owed him money! In fact, due to the application of tax credits both federally and provincially, Marshall was actually going to receive enough to finance a short honeymoon.

Now that he understood how the tax system could work in his favour, Marshall wanted to know more about what he had missed. Perhaps he could have claimed more, if he had known more about the rules. Had he only turned his tax files over to an advisor sooner!

THE PROBLEM

Tax is just one of those things. . .everyone has to deal with it; most people have difficulty doing so enthusiastically. While many pay an advisor to help them. . .they often pay their fees grudgingly. They perceive the entire experience like a double negative. . .the only thing worse than paying taxes is paying someone to figure out how much you have to pay!

How do you choose a tax advisor, someone with whom you'll have a long-term relationship in the quest to pay only the correct amount of tax over time. . .and not one cent more? How do you communicate with your tax advisor and learn the rules that can help you make tax-wise decisions all year long, and leverage the professional fees you are paying for tax help?

How do you turn the double negative around, to feel excited about your tax savings, and proud of the value you are getting from the dollars you pay to your tax advisor?

THE SOLUTION

You may be surprised at the solution to this dilemma. To find the right tax advisor you have to decide what it is that you want from the service you seek. There are numerous levels of tax-preparation, tax-accounting and tax-planning services to choose from in the marketplace. Which of these will best suit your needs today and into the future.

It goes without saying that every taxpayer who pays for a professional service expects a tax return that is 100% correct. However, there is a big difference between a return that is mathematically correct, and one that is done to your family's best advantage over the long term.

Find an advisor who will be as precious to your financial health as your doctor is to your physical health. Your tax advisor should be someone who knows you and your goals for your family and your business very well. S/he should be someone you trust implicitly, and who has earned your trust and respect by keeping up with the latest in tax law, and Revenue Canada's interpretation of the law, as well as your own personal, business and financial evolution.

In short, your professional tax advisor can be one of the most important people in your lifetime. For this reason, you should take some time to define this relationship carefully.

THE PARAMETERS

To find such a trusted advisor, consider this action plan:

- **Seek Referrals.** Ask your friends and business associates for referrals; check out the yellow pages and Chamber of Commerce or Board of Trade in your area for the names of well-respected tax advisors.
- **Expertise and Services Needed.** Find out what level of expertise you need: commercial tax preparation, accounting and auditing, corporate as well as personal returns, trust returns and estate planning.
- **Reputation and Experience.** Interview at least three professionals in your area. This can include independents, partners in a partnership, financial institutions, and so on. It's best to include one from every group to get the best overview of potential service, quality and price.
- **Ask Questions.** Come to the interview prepared to ask your top three taxation concerns.
- **Listen Well.** When you ask your questions, take note of the way the answers are communicated to you. Can you learn from this person? Is the person willing to help you learn? Is the person interested in you and your business? Does s/he make suggestions to you? Does s/he have a strong background in taxation?
- **Find Out About Service.** Ask about fees, guarantee of service, billing practices, errors or omissions insurance, size of organizations, additional services provided. What happens when errors occur?
- **Integrated Services.** Ask about the professional's ability to interact with others: lawyers, financial planners, insurance advisors and so on, should you need these services.
- **Make the Decision.** Choose the advisor you are most comfortable with.

- **Give a Trial.** Ask the advisor to complete a small job, to see if there is integrity behind the quality of the work, the ability to meet deadlines and to work with you on follow-up procedures.
- **Review the Accuracy of the Work.** Listen and learn as the advisor explains the results of the work to you.

Compile a "Top 10" list of questions to ask your advisor, such as:

1. What are the latest tax changes that will apply to my business operations this year?
2. What is the tax rate I will pay on each source of income I earn in the coming year?
3. What tax provisions should I be carrying forward from previous filing years?
4. What are the latest tax changes for our family unit to take advantage of?
5. How can our family members split income and transfer deductions and credits this year?
6. What are the retirement savings strategies we should be working towards?
7. How can we plan new investments outside our registered accounts to increase tax-deferred income sources?
8. How can we reduce tax withholding/tax instalment payments this year?
9. How should asset acquisitions and dispositions be timed to make the most tax sense?
10. What audit-proofing procedures should we be putting in place this year?

TAX ADVISOR

For those taxpayers who wish to come up to speed with their tax knowledge, and begin an education process with their advisors, consider the following list of recent tax provisions, for discussion purposes. We hope you find it helpful in unearthing new tax deductions and making sure there are no missed ones from the past. Take them along this tax season, together with your business and marketing plans.

TOP BUSINESS TAX CHANGES FOR UNINCORPORATED SMALL BUSINESSES IN 1998

Auto Expenses. For tax years 1998 and 1999, the Capital Cost Allowance (CCA) cost ceiling has for passenger vehicles has been increased to $26,000 (plus GST/PST/HST); lease payments maximum deductions are increased to $650 a month plus taxes and maximum interest deductions are $250 a month.

CPP Premiums

Remittances for employer–employee portion of premium payable increased in 1998.

Deduction for Health Care Premiums

The February 24, 1998, proposed to permit a business deduction for health care premiums paid by a small business. For fiscal periods ending after 1997, self-employed taxpayers or members of an unincorporated partnership can take a business deduction for premiums paid to a private health plan on behalf of the individual, his/her employees and his/her spouse or children. Certain restrictions apply in the case of employed family members. Note that in the case of a partnership the Adjusted Cost Base of a partnership interest must be reduced by the amount of private health services plan premiums that are deductible in the year.

EI Premium Holidays

To encourage private sector employers to hire young Canadians, the February 24, 1998, federal budget proposed to give employers an Employment Insurance premium holiday for additional young Canadians hired in 1999 and 2000. The 1998 year will be used as the base year in applying for premium relief, so employers must keep records of EI insurable earnings for 1998, as well as 1999 and 2000, in order to reap benefits.

Investment Tax Credits

Taxpayers will be required to add back to the credit any recaptured ITCs for any of the 10 preceding tax years.

Meal Expenses for Company Events

The 100% deduction status for meals and entertainment in cases where all employees participate in a company event, will be limited to six events in any calendar year, after February 23, 1998.

Meal Expenses for Remote Worksites

The 50% limitation on claiming the cost of meal expenses will not be required if meals are incurred by employers in respect of employees at remote worksites, or in cases where meals provided are for the general benefit of all employees; in short, the full amount of the expense in those cases will be deductible. The February 24, 1998, budget loosened the rules for remote worksites to include 100% deductibility for worksites which are at least 30 kilometres from the nearest urban area of at least 40,000 people if the employee is not expected to return daily to the principal residence.

Reserves

For those who switched their fiscal year ends to a calendar year end in 1995, prepare Form T1139, *Reconciliation of 1998 Business Income for Tax Purposes*, to make the 4th year reserve calculations. Take special note of the implications of certain changes in the taxpayer's circumstances: close or sale of business, emigration, bankruptcy or death — each can trigger unwanted income inclusion. It is therefore important to prepare tax-planning calculations to determine tax reduction strategies, like RRSP maximization and investment income diversification.

Year 2000 Computer Compliance

Accelerated CCA deductions of up to $50,000 will be allowed to small- and medium-sized business for the acquisition of computer hardware and software systems that replace those that are not Year 2000 compatible. The acquisitions will qualify for a 100% deduction of the eligible expenses, via an accelerated CCA claim. The assets must be Year 2000 compliant and acquired from January 1, 1998, to June 30, 1999. An election must be filed with the tax return to identify the property, its cost and date of acquisition. As well, the property being replaced must be described. Only unincorporated businesses or corporations not subject to the Large Corporations Tax will be eligible.

1998 Tax Deferral for Drought-Induced Sales of Breeding Livestock

Eligibility for this deferral is based on severe drought conditions (forage yields of less than 50% of long-term average over areas large enough to have impact on the industry). As of late 1998, there were 63 such areas in Saskatchewan and 27 areas in Alberta. (*Call The Jacks Institute for detailed information. 1-800-219-8889.*)

KEY FAMILY TAX CHANGES FOR 1998

Line 101: Employees. Those who receive certain taxable benefits, such as compensation from the employer for the financing of the costs of a new residence or losses on the sale of an old residence, must now report these as income.

Line 104: Volunteer Emergency Services Personnel. Income received by volunteer emergency services personnel will now be subject to a maximum offsetting deduction of up to $1000 **on line 229**.

Line 113: Old Age Security. Seniors will have received a small raise on their Old Age Security Payments, due to indexing but their Clawback threshold will not have been indexed to inflation.

Line 115: Private Pension Income. Seniors who receive benefits from the U.S. Social Security will be subject to new reporting rules. Claim the full amount of the benefits received, in Canadian funds, on Line 115 as income. Then take an offsetting tax deduction on Line 256 for 15% of these receipts.

Line 119: Employment Insurance Benefits. EI Recipients may be subject to an increased clawback of their benefits, depending on the number of weeks they have collected EI **after June 30, 1996**. See Line 235 for the computations.

Line 120: Interest Income. CSB Interest reporting has changed again in 1998. Series 43 will mature and must be reported for the final time.

Line 127: Capital Gains and Losses. Investors must be careful to apply gains and losses properly, especially in reducing mutual fund gains with their exempt gains balances, created with the February 22, 1994 election, and in recording tax loss selling from the volatile 1998 tax year. Small Business Corporation owners and those who own Qualifying Farm Properties still qualify for the $500,000 Capital Gains Exemption.

Line 129: RRSP Income. Those who receive severance packages will no longer be subject to minimum tax if these funds are transferred to an RRSP. **On the horizon in 1999,** there is good news for tax-free RRSP withdrawals for the disabled who buy accessible housing and for students who go back to school.

Line 130: Other Income. Income received from RESP withdrawals by a contributor must be included in income, but will now be subject to a special tax of 20%, unless the amounts are rolled into an RRSP. There must be sufficient RRSP Room for this option to be used.

Line 135:   The Self-Employed. Small business owners will also benefit from a new tax deduction for group health premiums, if they meet certain income and staffing requirements. In addition, there has been an increase in the amount that can be claimed in writing off an owned vehicle or a leased vehicle. There are also some restrictions in claiming meals and entertainment for staff of a small business.

Line 214:   Child Care Expenses. There are new rules for claiming Child Care Expenses. Parents will be happy to know the maximum claims have been increased to $7,000 for each child under 7 and $4,000 for children age 7-16. Special claims can also be made for disabled children.

Line 219:   Moving Expenses. This year, there is even more good news for those who move, as deductible expenses can include some of the costs of carrying an unsold residence.

Line 307:   Personal Amount Supplement. There is a new supplement to the Basic Personal Amount, of up to $250 in 1998; $500 in 1999. This will affect numerous calculations on the return, including the claim for tuition and education credits, the spousal amount, and other calculations influenced by the "tax free zone."

Line 308:   CPP premiums have been increased for 1998 and will continue to increase into the foreseeable future.

Line 312:   EI premiums decreased from the year before and will decrease again in 1999.

Line 315:   The Caregiver Amount. This new credit is available to those who take care of a parent or grandparent age 65 years or older, or a relative at least 18 years of age who is dependent due to mental or physical infirmity, in a dwelling in which the supporting person and the dependant lived.

Line 316:   The Disability Amount. This is now claimable based on the verification of occupational therapists and psychologists.

Line 319:   Interest Paid on Student Loans. There is also a new tax credit for loan interest paid on student loans that features a 5-year carry-forward feature for unused amounts, starting in 1998.

Line 323: The Tuition and Education Amounts. Education tax credits have been increased for full-time students to $200 a month; there is also a new education tax credit for part-time students of $60 a month. One or the other may be claimed for a month but not both. The part-time credit may also affect the ability for a high-income spouse to claim child care expenses on Line 214.

Line 326: Amounts Transferred from Spouse. The amounts that can be transferred from spouse may be affected by the Personal Amount Supplement.

Line 330: **Medical Expenses.** Medical expense claims have also been enhanced: one can now claim reasonable expenses for training in connection with providing care to an infirm dependant.

Line 413: Labour-sponsored funds tax credit. This credit has been enhanced for investors in the 1998 tax year.

Line 418: Additional tax on RESP Accumulated Income Payments. This line provides a place for taxpayers to pay tax on RESP earnings, when the beneficiary does not go to school.

Line 419: The individual surtax. This tax on federal tax has been reduced for low- and middle-income earners in 1998 and future years.

Line 428/ Provincial taxes and credits. There are numerous changes to
479: provincial tax calculations and credits. Many provinces now have their own Child Tax Benefit.

IMPORTANT BUSINESS TAX CHANGES FOR 1997

Auto Expenses

The CCA cost ceiling was increased to $25,000 (plus taxes); lease payments maximum deductions were reduced to $550 a month (plus taxes) and interest deductions to a maximum of $250 a month. After December 31, 1996, the calculations of eligible leasing costs for passenger vehicles were increased to $29,412. This figure, plus taxes, or the manufacturer's list price, whichever is more, multiplied by 85% was used in the calculation.

Bankruptcy

Where the fiscal period of the business ends after the date of bankruptcy, income from the business, including all reserve amounts, would be reported on the post-bankruptcy return. The Finance Department also announced that unremitted source deductions and unpaid GST/HST will take priority over all other debts of a taxpayer in such cases.

Fiscal Year End Reserve Calculations

1997 was the third year in the 10-year transitional period and a maximum reserve of 75% of the stub period income could be claimed.

Harmonized Sales Taxes

HST became effective in NB, NS and NF in April, 1997; the federal sales tax component is 7%; the provincial component is 8%.

NISA

Changes were made to the application and administration of the NISA funds for farmers and tax filing in general. The Statement of Farming Activities and the NISA forms were combined, and Revenue Canada now acts as the information centre for the Ministry of Agriculture. A new tax guide, Farming Income and NISA includes Form T1163 Statement A, *NISA Account Information and Statement of Farming Activities for Individuals,* which must be filed by June 15 of the year following the end of the taxation year. This form is used for tax-filing purposes, and it must be filed on time with your tax return.

New Deadlines for NISA Applicants

For NISA purposes, the new tax forms will be accepted until December 31, but then the maximum entitlement will be reduced by 5% per month after June 15. Form T1164 Statement B must be filed for each additional farming operation. Producers of edible horticulture commodities in the province of Ontario will complete Form T1165, *Statement of Farming Activities for Ontario Self-Directed Risk Management.* Farmers who are not currently participating in NISA and do not wish to do so in the future, will continue to file Form T2042, *Statement of Farming Income.* The NISA Administrative Cost Share of $55 is deductible as a carrying charge on line 221.

Tax Deferral on 1997 Income from Drought-Induced Sales

Owners of breeding livestock in certain areas of Saskatchewan and Manitoba who were forced to sell herd animals because of drought conditions could defer income from those sales for one year. There were 79 areas in Saskatchewan and 41 areas in Manitoba.

Frequency of Source Deduction Remittances for Small Business

Those employers with average monthly withholding amounts of less than $1,000 for the second preceding calendar year, and who have no compliance problems in either their withholding account or GST/HST accounts, for the preceding 12 months can now choose to remit their source deductions withheld from employees on a quarterly rather than a monthly basis. These remittances would be required on March 31, June 30, September 30 and December 31. The remittances are due the 15th of the month following the end of each quarter.

Filing Deadlines for Investment Tax Credits

New credits claimed after February 18, 1997, must be filed within 12 months of the filing due date for the year in which property was acquired.

Refunds of EI Premiums

Employers who faced large premium increases in Employment Insurance because of the government's switch to an hours-based, first-dollar coverage system, could obtain a refund for 1997 and 1998 for a part of the increases at the time when the T4 Summary information was filed.

Film and Video Production Services Support

The film and video industry received an extension on foreign film production service tax shelters to October 1997 on the new matchable expense rules. Also, the existing Canadian Film or Video Production Tax Credit was extended to allow a greater range of productions, including foreign film production, to qualify for eligible Canadian labour expenses incurred after October 1997, provided that the production is not a tax shelter.

Director's Liability for Unremitted Source Deductions

A Federal Court of Appeal decision (Soper v. The Queen) has suggested that directors who are not involved in day-to-day decision making of a corporation may make a successful defence against personal liability by demonstrating due diligence and a reasonable degree of skill and care. Personal knowledge and background will be taken into account.

IMPORTANT BUSINESS TAX CHANGES FOR 1996

Business Number

All businesses were required to conform to a new Business Number starting January 1, 1997. This number is used for all payroll remittances, the GST/HST, corporate income tax and import/export accounts.

CCA on Canadian Film Productions

Starting in 1996, the old CCA deduction was replaced by a fully refundable tax credit, called a Canadian Film Credit, for eligible films produced by qualified taxable Canadian corporations. This credit is 25% of eligible salaries and wages expended after 1994 by a qualified corporation, as long as the amounts don't exceed 48% of the cost of production. To qualify, the production must be certified by the Minister of Canadian Culture.

Depreciable Property Rules

A new "Stop-loss" rule was introduced for the transfer of depreciable property by a corporation, trust or partnership whose tax cost was greater than the proceeds of disposition. If the transferor or someone "affiliated" with the transferor — including the spouse — has a right to acquire the property within 30 days, the loss on disposition may not be recognized until a subsequent circumstance. This includes a change in the property's use to non-income-producing or a disposition to a person not affiliated with the transferor. The transferor will, however, be able to claim CCA after the transfer on the difference between the transferred property's tax cost and the transferor's proceeds of disposition.

Fiscal Year End Reserve Calculations

1996 was the second year in the 10-year transitional period and a maximum reserve of 85% of the stub period income could be claimed.

Western Grain Transition Payments

Where a taxpayer sold farmland before receiving the Western Grain Transition Payment, the amount receivable was used to reduce the ACB of the land immediately before disposition.

Tax–Exempt Kilometres Paid to Employees

An employer could deduct 33 cents for the first 5,000 kilometres and 27 cents for each kilometre thereafter, paid to employees who use their personal vehicles in the business. The amounts are 5 cents a kilometre higher in the Yukon and North West Territories.

RECAP: Ten Skill Testing Questions to Discuss With Your Advisors

True   False?

1. ❑   ❑   If you can start a viable business venture, you'll be able to diversify income sources, defer the reporting of taxable income, and split income with family members.

True. Any investment advisor will tell you that the way to spread risk and accumulate wealth is to pay close attention to your asset mix. You want to earn income from a variety of sources: employment or self-employment, pensions, dividends, capital gains, interest and so on. When you start a small business, you'll be creating two types of income: ongoing profits from the operations of the venture; and the potential for capital gains on the future sale of your business. This is a great way to diversify your taxable income sources, defer taxation of accrued wealth into the future and reduce your overall tax burden through income-splitting with family members.

True   False?

2. ❑   ❑   A myriad of tax deductions that fall under very loose statutory guidelines are available to the self-employed.

True. Business owners are only taxed on net profits, which are added to taxable income annually, and taxed at the appropriate marginal tax rate. The rules governing tax deductibility of expenditures are very general, and found in about a half a dozen sections of the Income Tax Act. They centre around two basic concepts: your ability to explain to a tax auditor why the expense you wish to deduct was reasonable under the circumstances, and how it was used to create income for your business, which has a reasonable expectation of profit, now or in the future. You must also show the auditor that any personal use component of the expenditure has been removed.

True False?

3. ❑   ❑   The self-employed can't write off the value of their own labour.

That's true of unincorporated small businesses. (Within a corporation, you can hire yourself and write off your salary like that of any other employee.) However, you have to think of the positive side of that equation. . .you're not paying tax on the equity you are building in your business either. Every hour you spend growing your business counts towards the appreciating value of your business on a tax-deferred basis. So while the proprietor cannot write off the value of his/her own labour, take comfort in the fact that your appreciating equity in the business will never be taxed until you sell your business. . .and then, if you set things up properly, by forming a small business corporation, your gains could be completely tax-free.

True False?

4. ❑   ❑   The self-employed are stuck financing all the risk of building their business, without tax relief.

Not so. Here's why. What is your most precious commodity? Is it your time? Your money? Your health? Likely it's all of those things. The key to preserving your resources is to use them wisely; to multiply them if possible, and to have them work for you. A small business provides you with the vehicle to leverage time, money and human resources needed to build appreciating equity over time. And best of all, the costs of leveraging — hiring staff, paying interest on an operating loan, leasing computers, marketing your services — are tax deductible, if you earn income from your venture, which has a reasonable expectation of profit, and keep proper records.

True False?

5. ❑   ❑   It's much better to arrange for one person in the family to earn $50,000 than for two people to earn $25,000.

False. If you understand a little about our tax system, you'll know it's best to minimize realized income in the hands of one taxpayer and to "spread the wealth" into the hands of many. The taxpayer who earns $50,000 pays tax at a marginal rate of about 40%. The $25,000-earner pays tax at about 26%. The potential return on the process of income splitting is 14%, a pretty good return on your tax-planning investment; *and* it's legal. You'll want to strive to split income with your family members. In fact, by starting a home-based business, you have the potential to reap double-digit returns in tax savings, simply by giving family members an opportunity to work for you.

True   False?

6. ❑   ❑   Keeping up with tax law and its continuous change is a pointless effort.

False. Most Canadians have the educational qualifications to understand their own tax system. Motivation to understand it and use it to their advantage, is often a bigger problem, which is puzzling. True, it is not possible for every taxpayer to be a tax expert. That's not your goal, nor was it the goal of this book to make you one. (I'm sure you're relieved.)

However, the essence of opportunity lies within the structure of our tax system: It is based on voluntary compliance and self-assessment. It is your legal right and duty to arrange your affairs within the framework of the law to report the least amount of tax possible. By learning more about the existing provisions within our Income Tax Act, you'll be empowered to make tax-wise decisions throughout the year. Your motivation to do so? Simple. . .it's money; *your money.*

True   False?

7. ❑   ❑   Small business owners can reap tax savings of 26% to over 50% on each an every dollar they spend in their small business ventures, depending on their province of residence and income levels.

Yes. Because each qualifying business expenditure reduces business income dollar for dollar, you'll reap double-digit returns for each receipt you keep. It's important to know the income parameters you need to reach to maximize the return on your expenditures, and how each different income source you earn will be taxed in the future.

True   False?

8. ❑   ❑   The cost of your computer purchase can be written off in full against business revenues.

False. Many business owners fail to classify their expenditures into two main categories: operating expenses and capital expenditures. This error can be expensive in a tax audit. The former are 100% deductible against revenues of the business, and can even be used to create a loss. In all businesses (excluding those who own an investment property), capital cost allowances, the partial deduction allowed for the wear and tear on depreciable assets, can increase an operating loss. So your computer will be written off over a period of years — unless it is a Year 2000 compliance purchase, in which case you will qualify for a 100% write off in the period January 1, 1998, to June 1, 1999.

True   False?

9. ❑   ❑   It's difficult to justify claims for car and in-home business workspaces.

No, it's really quite easy to comply. All you have to do is separate your personal use of the assets from your business use. In the case of the auto, this is done by keeping a distance log which reports all your driving for both business and personal purposes. At the end of the tax year all expenses relating to the vehicle are totalled, and prorated according to the business kilometres driven divided by the total kilometres driven in the year. A similar process, based on square footage of the workspace in the home over the total living area, will help you claim the properly deductible portions of home expenses. The recordkeeping process can be easily recorded in your Daily Business Journal.

True   False?

10. ❑   ❑   Most taxpayers lose their tax audit appeals when they go to court.

Unfortunately this is true. Revenue Canada wins appeals at the Tax Court level about 68% of the time.* However, the odds for winning are much better locally. Appealing under a Notice of Objection to the Chief of Appeals in your area reaps a 90% successful conclusion result. This negotiated approach to solving taxes in dispute, can pay off for both

* At the time of writing.

parties, particularly when it comes to the grey areas of the law. For that reason, taxpayers should never back away from filing a Notice of Objection to a reassessment of their taxes, if they believe their tax return was correct as filed.

CONCLUSION:

Most taxpayers in Canada — 95% — voluntarily comply with the law to self-assess their income and pay taxes. This would indicate that Canadians have a very high respect for their tax system. Unfortunately, it is the minority who fail to comply with the law who make compliance and enforcement activities a necessity. Even Revenue Canada finds the process difficult, as stated in their document *Compliance: From Vision to Strategy*.

"Ensuring compliance. . .is an ongoing challenge. It requires credible enforcement strategies that are seen to protect honest taxpayers by making sure those who cheat are caught."

Roderick Hill and Muhammed Kabir of the Department of Economics, University of New Brunswick, conducted a study for the Canadian Tax Foundation in 1996. Their research discovered the following:

- That underground economy growth between 1964 and 1995 was estimated to be between 3 and 11% of Gross Domestic Product.

- That the growth in the underground economy is due to changes in both direct taxes, like personal income taxes and payroll taxes, and indirect taxes, such as the GST.

- That the changes to the GST have contributed to the growth of the underground economy.

- That rapid growth in the underground economy was noted in the late 1960s and early 1970s, a period of tax reform in Canada, and again in the period since 1987, another period of tax reform in this country. In fact, according to the research, there has been as much growth in the underground economy in the period 1989 to 1995 as in the previous 20-year period.

- A Quebec survey on underground labour market activities found that 8.5% of respondents reported underground work with average earnings of about $2,000. This is significant as it concluded that there were high participation rates in the underground economy for low-income people including students, the unemployed, those on social assistance and unmarried people. ("The Effect of Taxes on

Labor Supply in the Underground Economy." Lemieux, Fortin, Frechette in *The American Economic Review,* 1994.)

- The authors of the study concluded: ". . .there is very strong evidence that tax rates, defined in a wide variety of ways, have significantly influenced currency demand and presumably the extent of tax-evading underground activity in Canada during the last 30 years. Tax rate changes have increased the size of the Underground Economy, and that increase has become relatively rapid in the last 10 years. Revenue Canada's concern about tax evasion and the underground economy appears well justified."

Therefore, one of the solutions to fighting the Underground Economy is the reduction in overall direct and indirect taxes that Canadians are subject to in the future. Another is the support of audit activity by the business community, in the quest to promote fairness, equity, and a level playing field.

George Bernard Shaw, perhaps unwittingly, captured the essence of the entrepreneurial spirit in his memorable saying: "You see things; and you say, 'Why?' But I dream things that never were; and I say, 'Why not?'"

This phrase perhaps best describes the ultimate conflict between the taxpayer and the taxman. *The taxman sees what is, and assesses accordingly; the taxpayer sees what could be, and files a tax return accordingly.*

What's important is that average Canadians know and understand that the law is on their side. To make sure your expenditures are tax deductible, you must be prepared to challenge Revenue Canada's interpretation of your tax-filing profile, and make those grey areas of the law work in your favour. Some, in fact, can even turn a tax audit into a profitable experience.

Ultimately it is in the commitment to the self-assessment system that Canadian small business owners have the best hope for fairness and efficiency in tax compliance matters. Taxpayers must be trusted to report their income and deductions honestly, and they must have numerous opportunities to work within the framework of the law to correct errors and omissions in order to comply with the law. And, when it comes to the taxpayer's relationship with a tax auditor, it is important for all parties to observe this basic right as encoded in the Declaration of Taxpayer Rights:

"You are entitled to be presumed honest unless there is evidence to the contrary."

Index

About Evelyn Jacks

Evelyn Jacks is the Founder and President of The Jacks Institute, a national private career college specializing in tax and business-related courses for tax industry professionals. She is the author of over 25 best-selling books on personal income tax preparation, and has written more than 75 industry-related training courses. Evelyn is a frequent national commentator on federal and provincial budgets and has criss-crossed Canada to answer your tax questions on local and national TV and radio programs. She is a well-known speaker to numerous industry groups, including financial planners, insurance advisors and the tax accounting community. She has recently been named one of Canada's National Entrepreneurs of the Year.

Books by Evelyn Jacks:

Jacks on Tax Savings: Everyone's Favourite Canadian Tax Guide to Preparing Income Tax Returns. 15th Anniversary Edition.

201 Easy Ways to Reduce Your Taxes. 6th edition.

The Canadian Home Business Guide to Tax Savings. 2nd edition.

Jacks on Personal Finance: Modern Money Management for Utterly Confused Canadians. 1st edition.

Make Sure It's Deductible. 1st edition.

Jacks on GST: The Authoritative Guide for Business and Consumers.

Certificate Courses from The Jacks Institute

Begin a new career as a qualified income tax preparer. Courses are available by self-study on your home computer; books and tax training software included in the tax deductible tuition fees. Software versions include CANTAX Pro, HOMETAX Pro and L'Impôt Personnel for those in the province of Quebec. Payroll and bookkeeping courses feature Simply Accounting.

The Quick and Easy Tax Course: A basic income-tax preparation course for beginners, designed to train students to prepare their own simple income tax returns, or those of friends and family using a home computer.

The Intermediate Personal Income Tax Preparation Course: A professional entry-level course designed to train the student to prepare tax returns for others, for a fee, out of their own home or office, or to gain employment with tax accounting or financial-planning firms.

The Advanced Income Tax Preparation Course: An advanced course for those who wish to prepare multi-tiered tax returns and do tax-planning scenarios by computer. Experience preparing income tax returns by computer is an asset.

The Personal Tax and Money Management Course: This informative course features over a dozen tax-planning forms and procedures to teach you to help your family, clients or associates plan to save money through tax wise decision making during the tax year.

Income Tax Preparation for Small Business: For unincorporated business ventures, a detailed course on tax-filing provisions required for small businesses, including statement preparation, capital acquisitions and dispositions and operational deductions.

The Computerized Payroll Clerk Course: A skill-oriented course that teaches payroll preparation, T4 Slip preparation and month-end reporting with an emphasis on tax requirements of the employer.

The Computerized Bookkeeping Course: The right course for every small business owner, his/her spouse or other family member, who seeks to learn how to prepare financial statements by computer in order to make proper business decisions and meet the requirements of Revenue Canada.

The TaxBiz Tax Update Course: Especially for experienced tax professionals, a thorough, skill-testing update on the latest tax changes for the upcoming tax season.

Taxation in a Global Economy Course: Learn the tax rules in place for those who regularly travel the globe: from young mobile and skilled workers to snowbirds, vacationers with property in other countries, emigrants, non-residents and immigrants. An especially important course in light of the new emphasis on foreign asset reporting.

A special offer
for readers of Evelyn Jacks' Best-selling Tax Guides:
ENQUIRE TODAY ABOUT YOUR FREE BROCHURE
(Never an Obligation)

from
THE JACKS INSTITUTE
Canada's Leading Trainer of Tax Industry Professionals

Featuring

CERTIFICATE TRAINING COURSES BY SELF-STUDY
for individuals, professional firms and educational institutes.

To Thank You For Your Interest In Tax Savings
Receive A $50 Gift Certificate
*To be used towards any tax-deductible, certificate course
from The Jacks Institute.* Simply call, write, e-mail or mail your
request for the gift certificate and a free brochure. Contact:*

The Jacks Institute at our Internet Campus: www.jackstax.com
or
phone: (local) 204-956-7161   (toll free) 1-800-219-8889
or
fax: complete form below and send to 204-949-9429

Your Name_____

Address _____

City _____

Province _____   PostalCode _____

E-mail _____   Fax _____

Phone (H) (_____)_____   (W) (_____)_____

The Jacks Institute, 401-177 Lombard Avenue, Winnipeg, Manitoba R3B 0W5
*Proof of purchase is required. Not good with any other certificates or offers.
 One offer per person only.

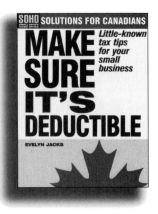